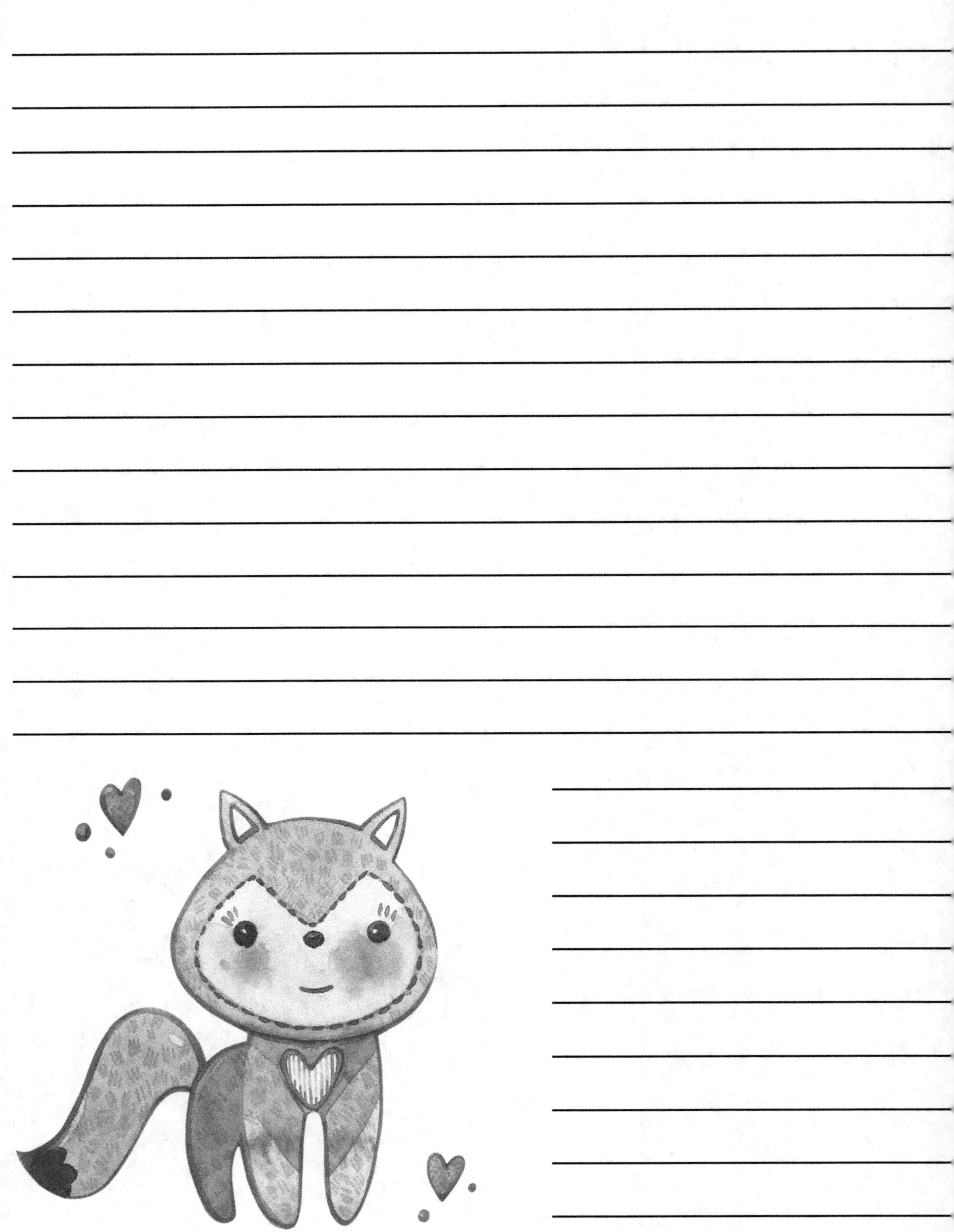

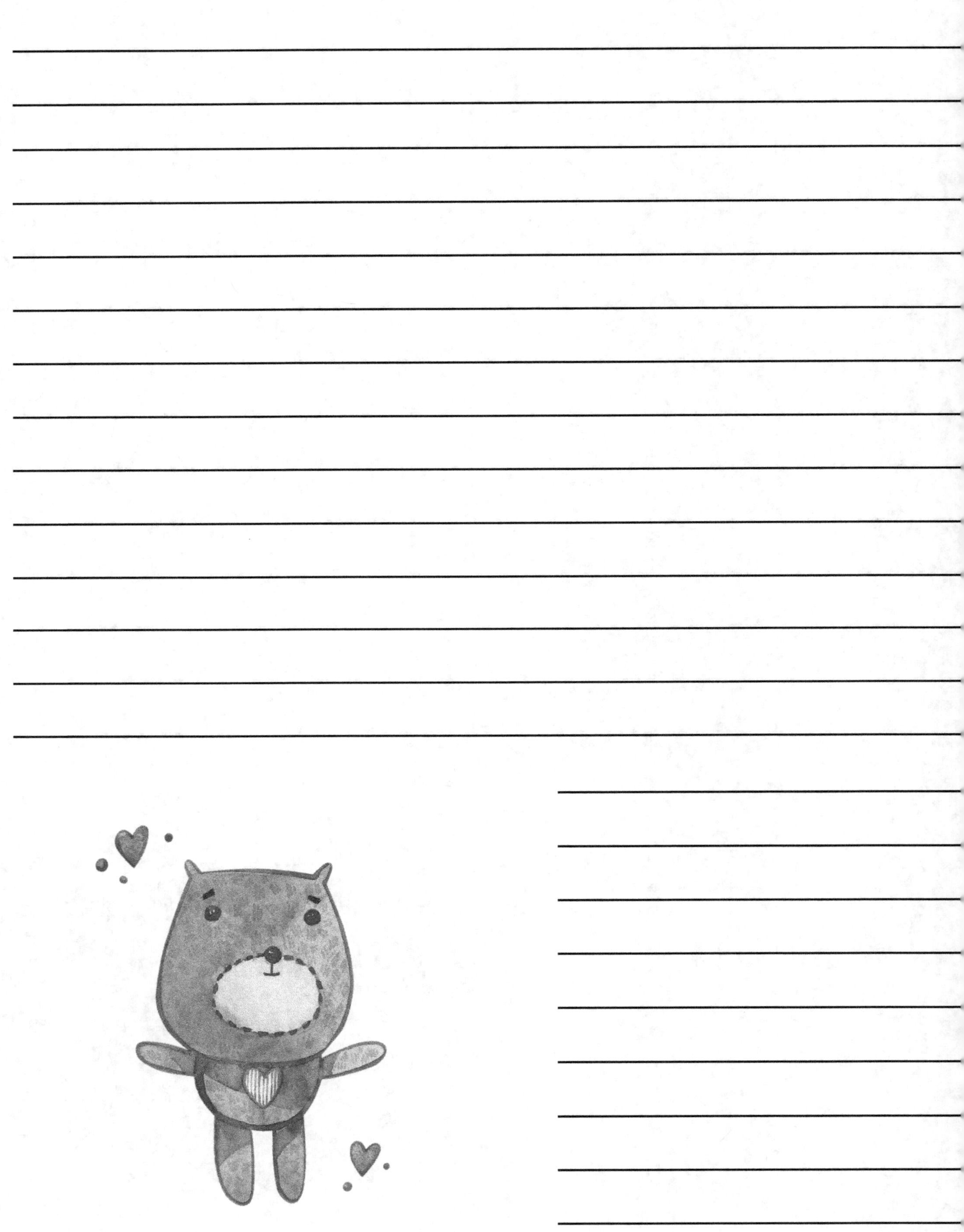

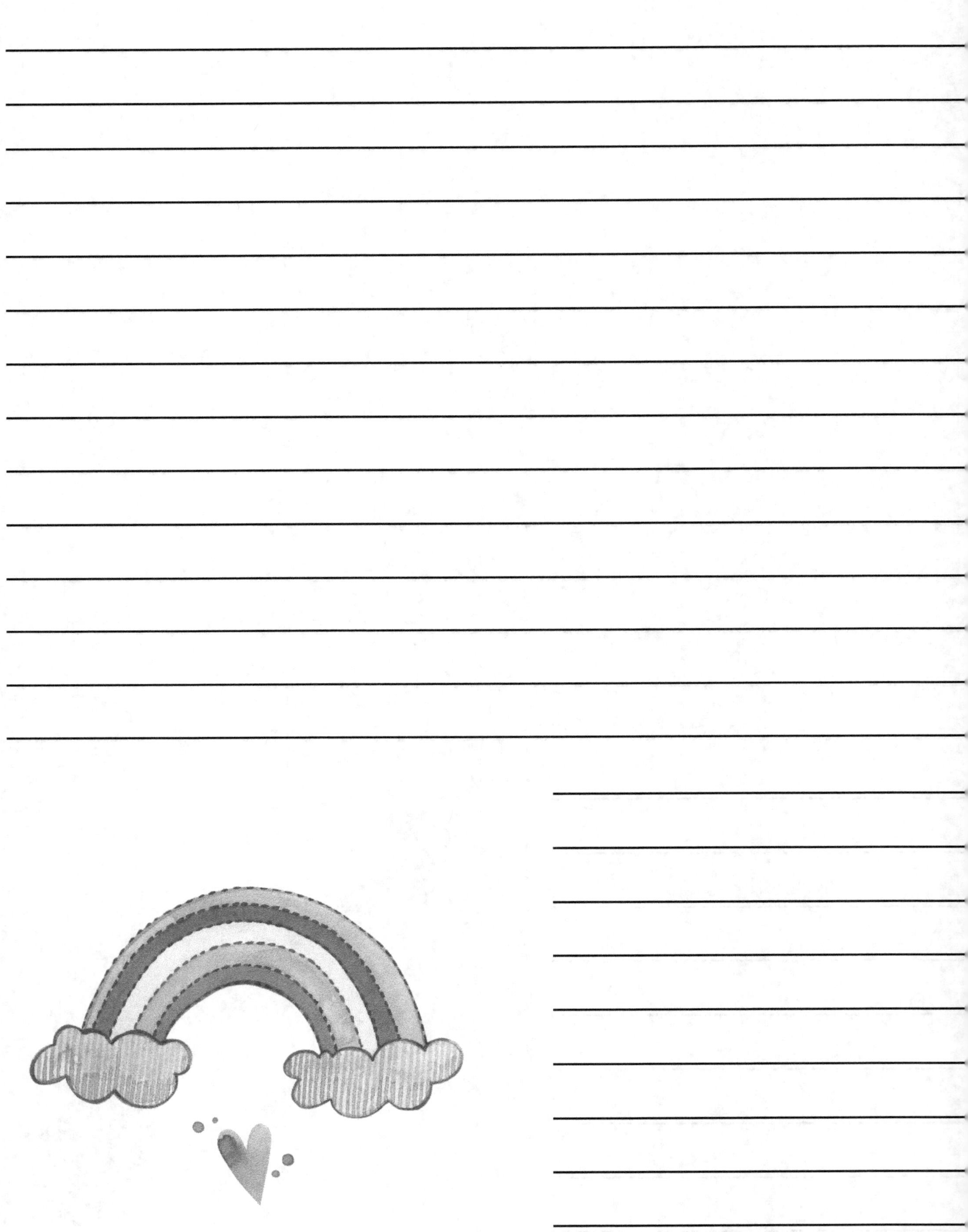

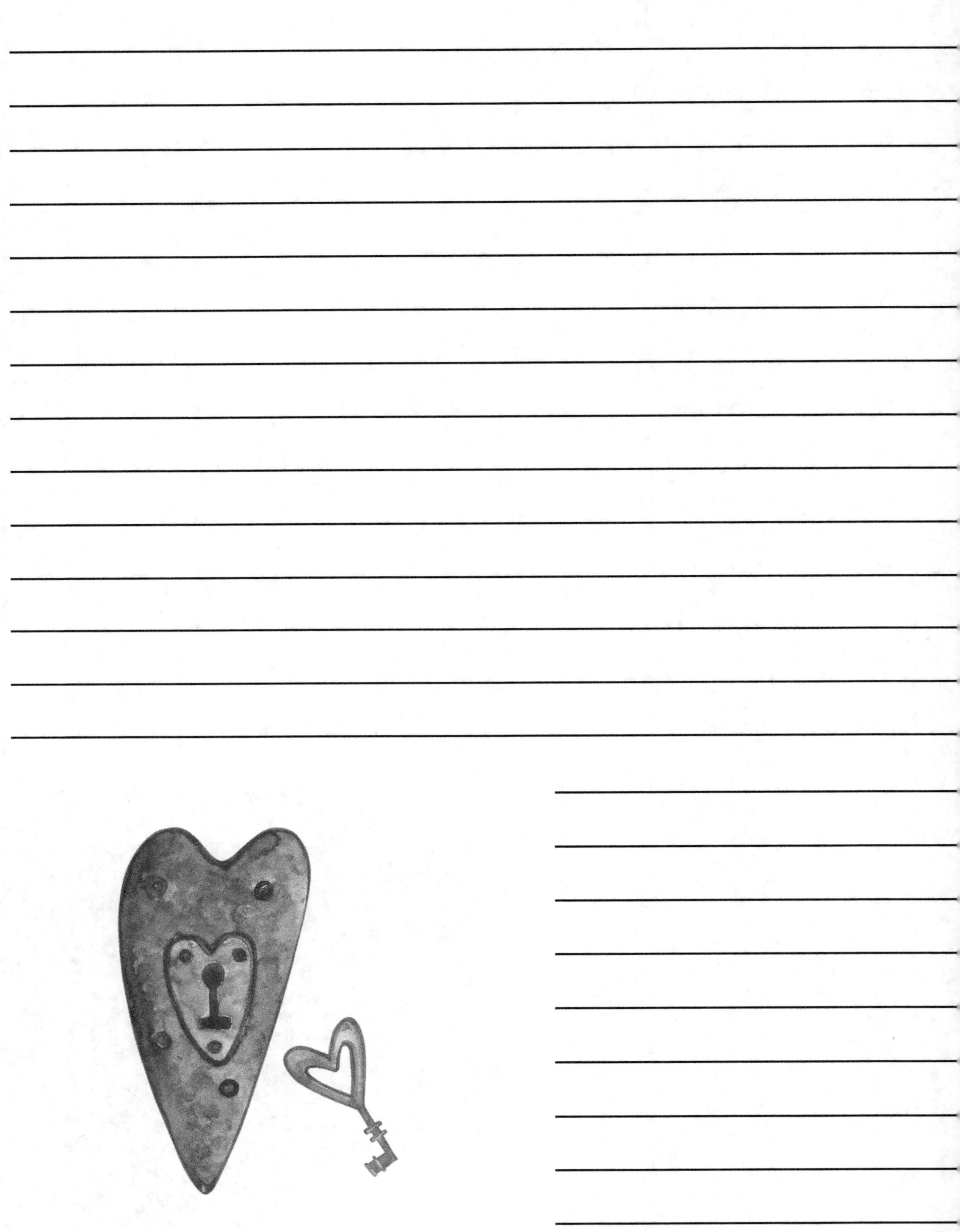

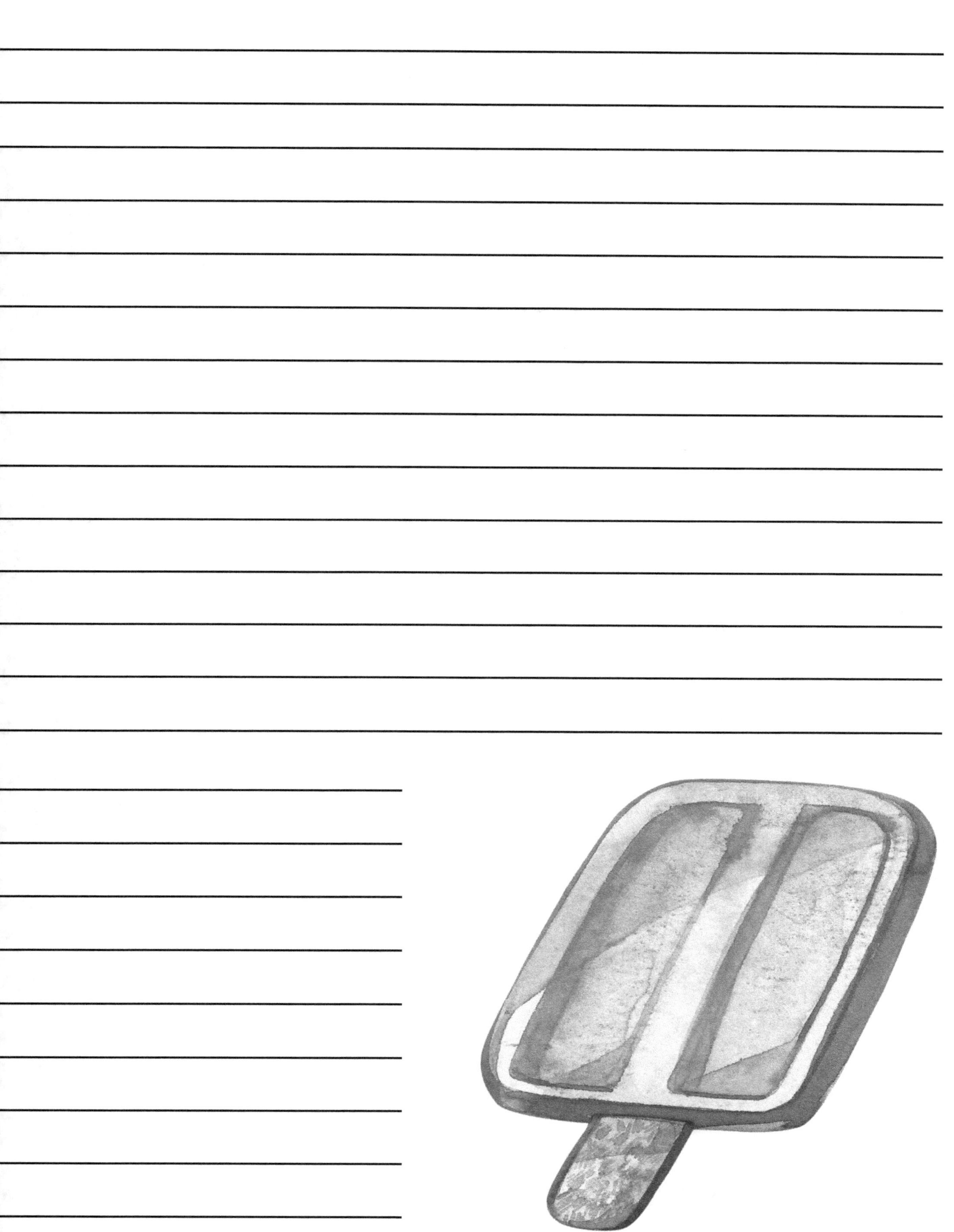

you
+
me
=
love

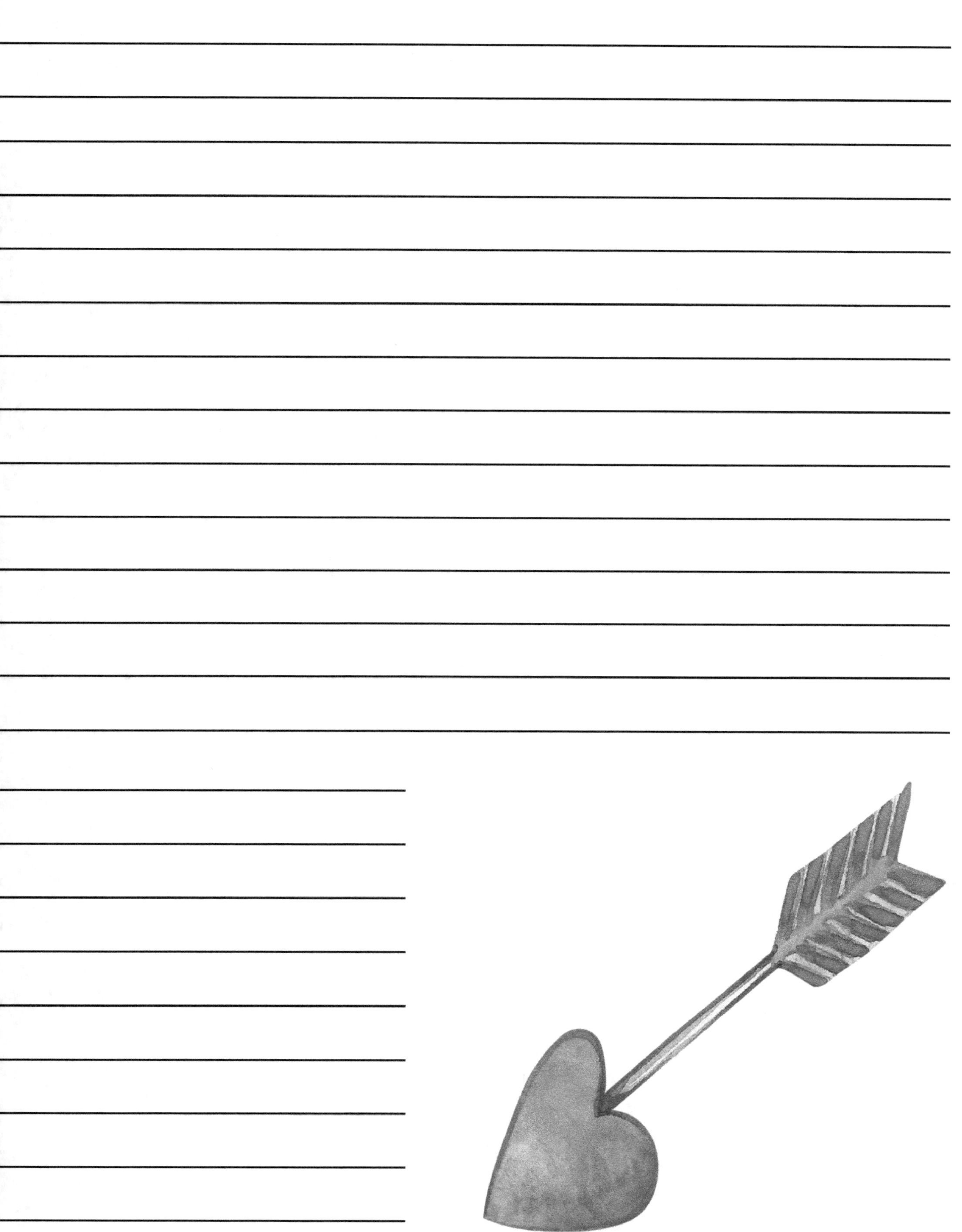

i love you

Love you

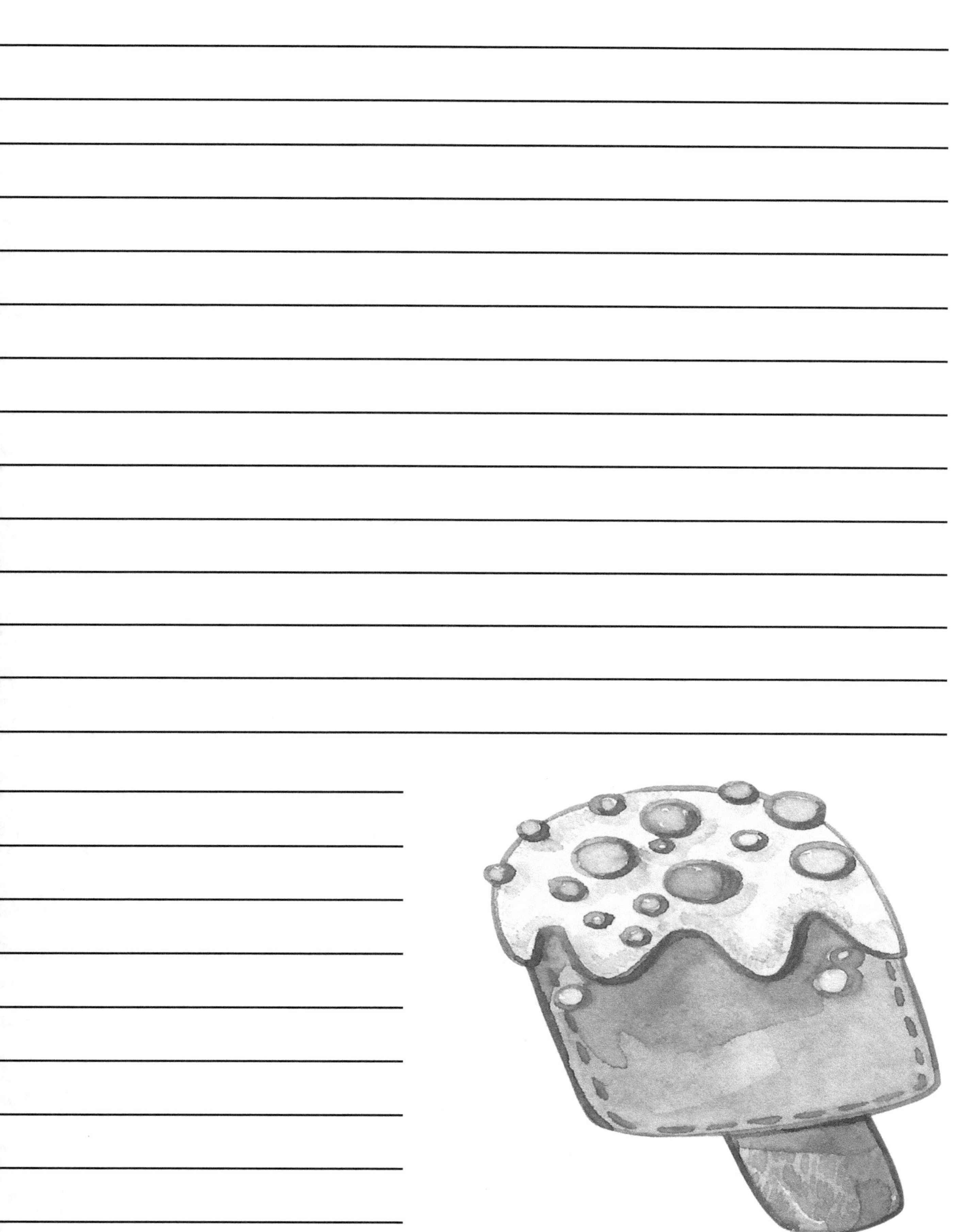

LOVE

you are loved

love
is all
you
need

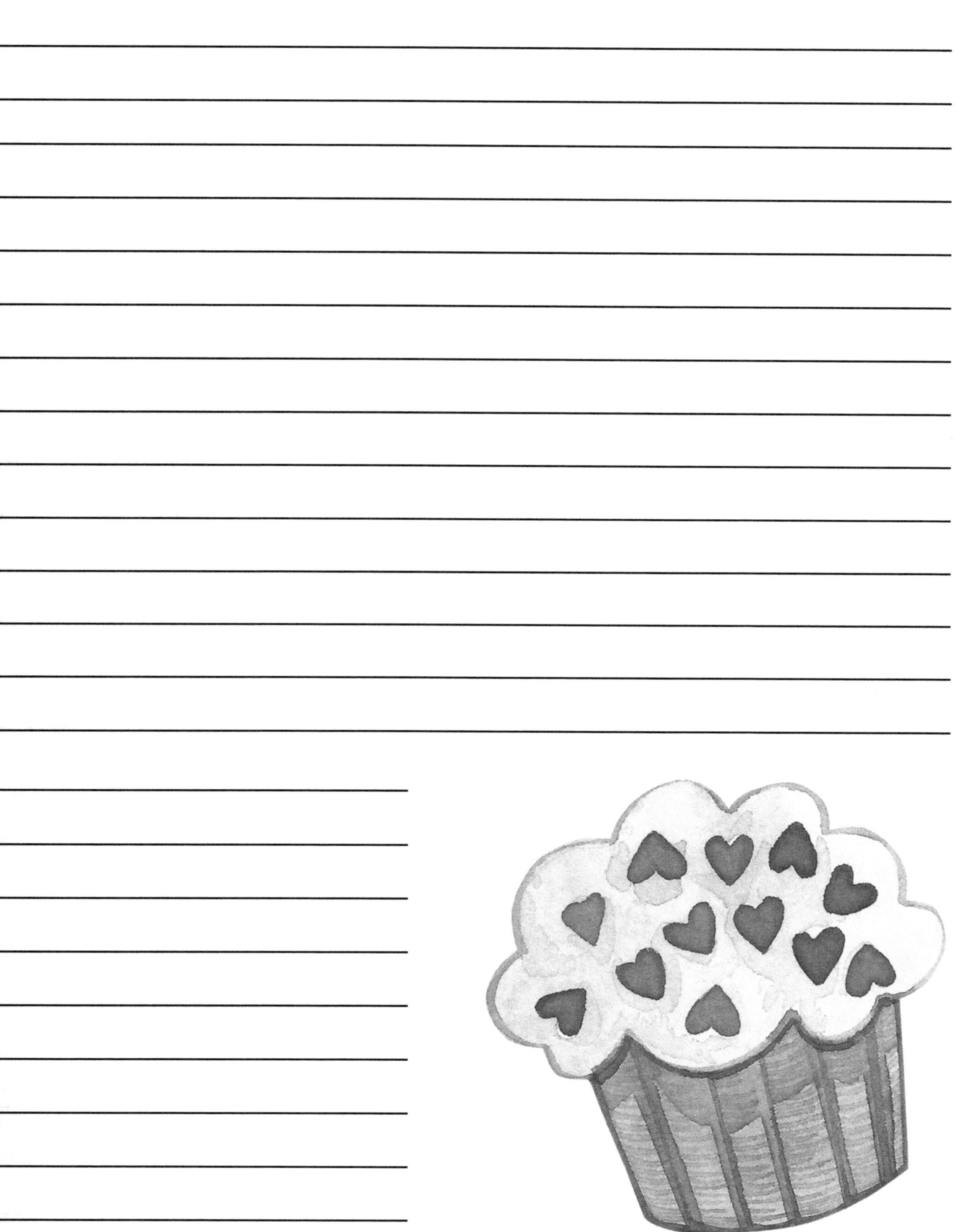

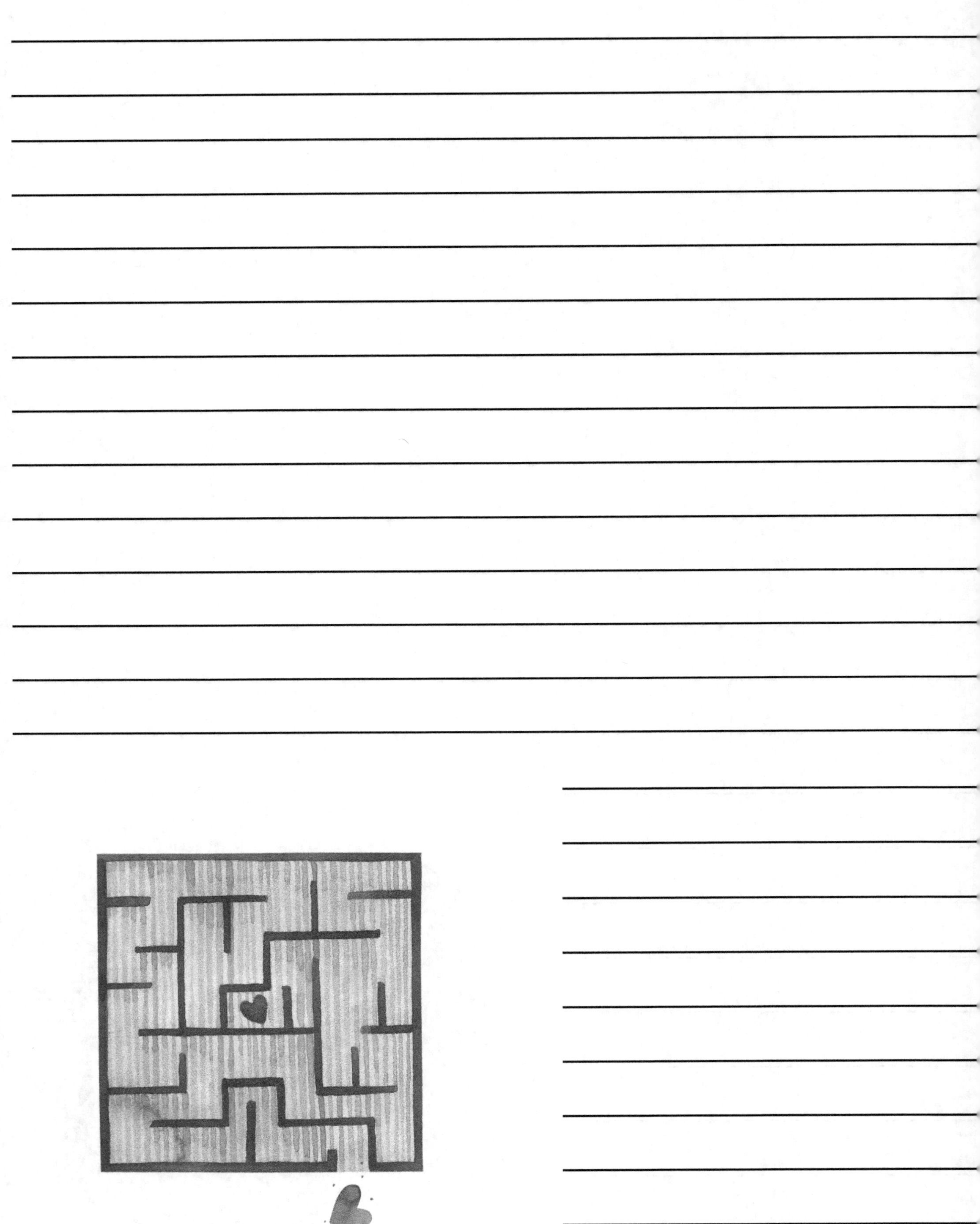

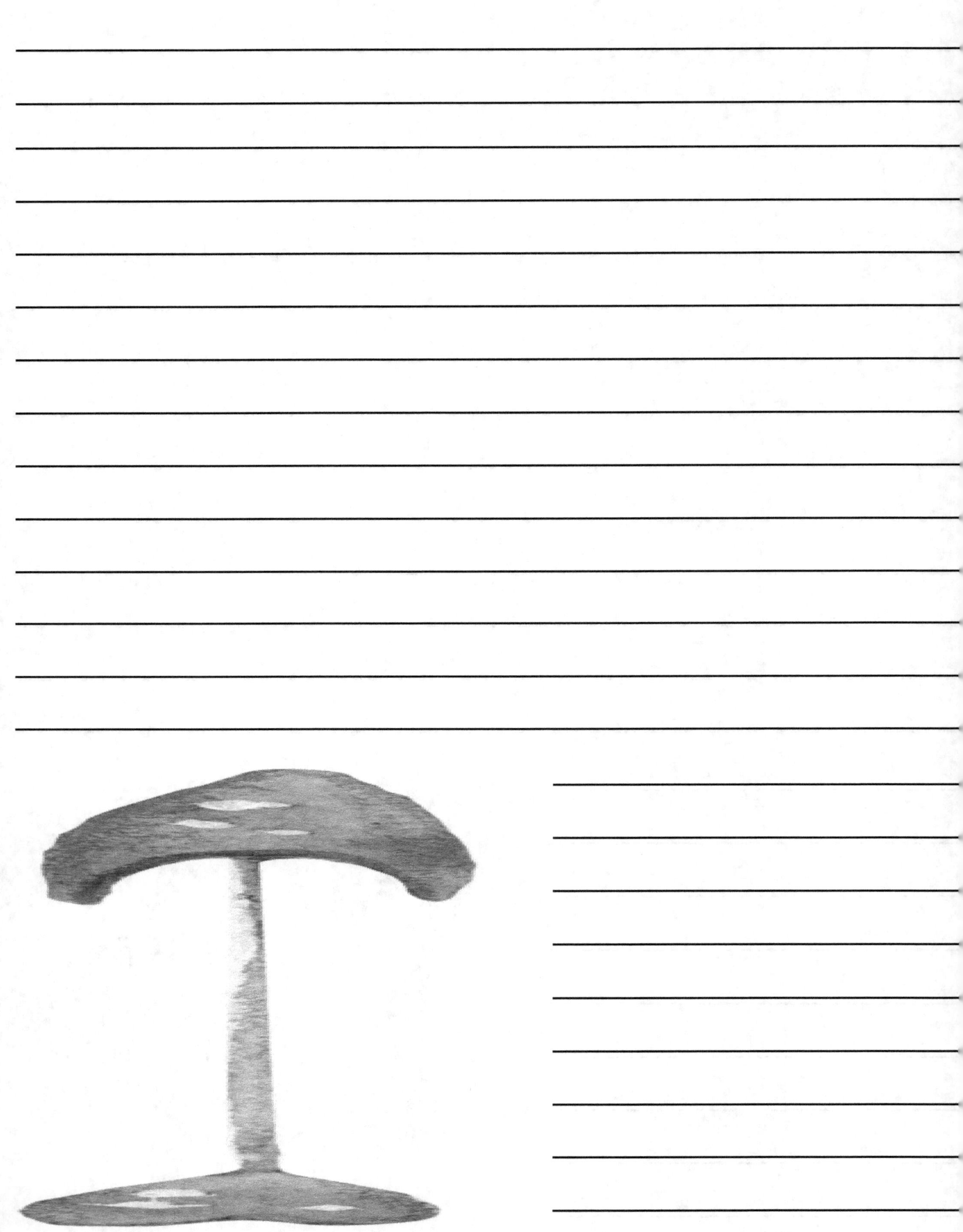

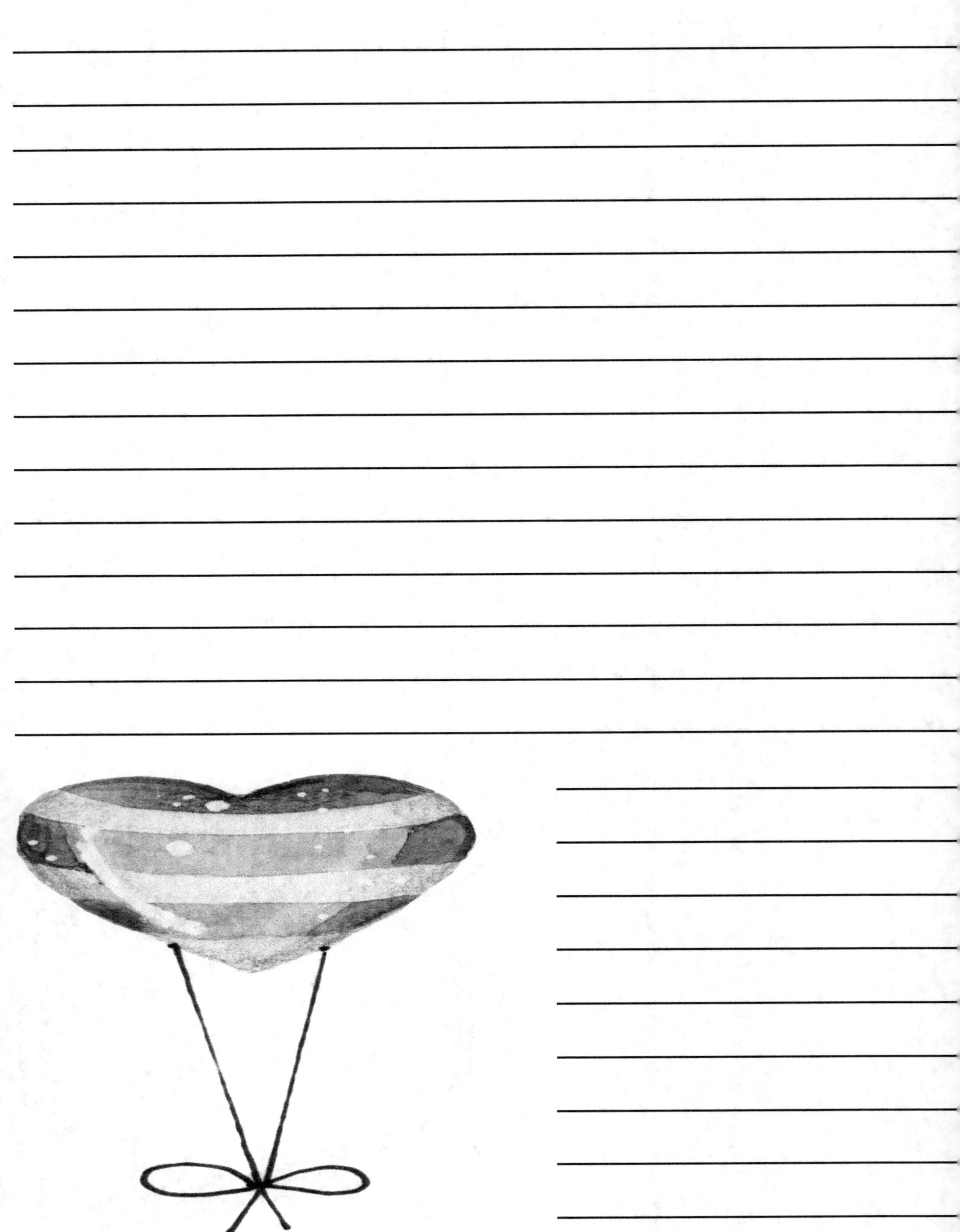

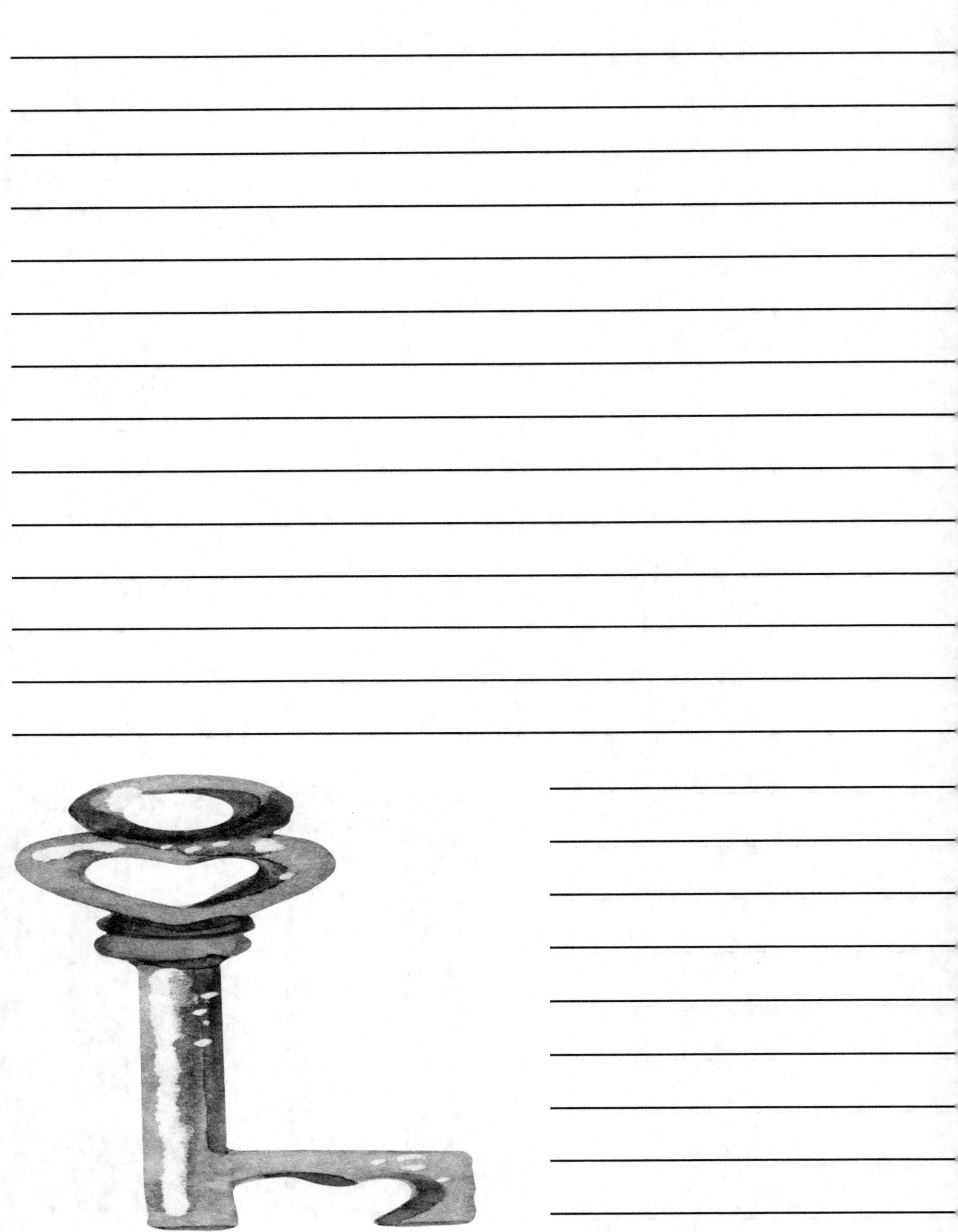

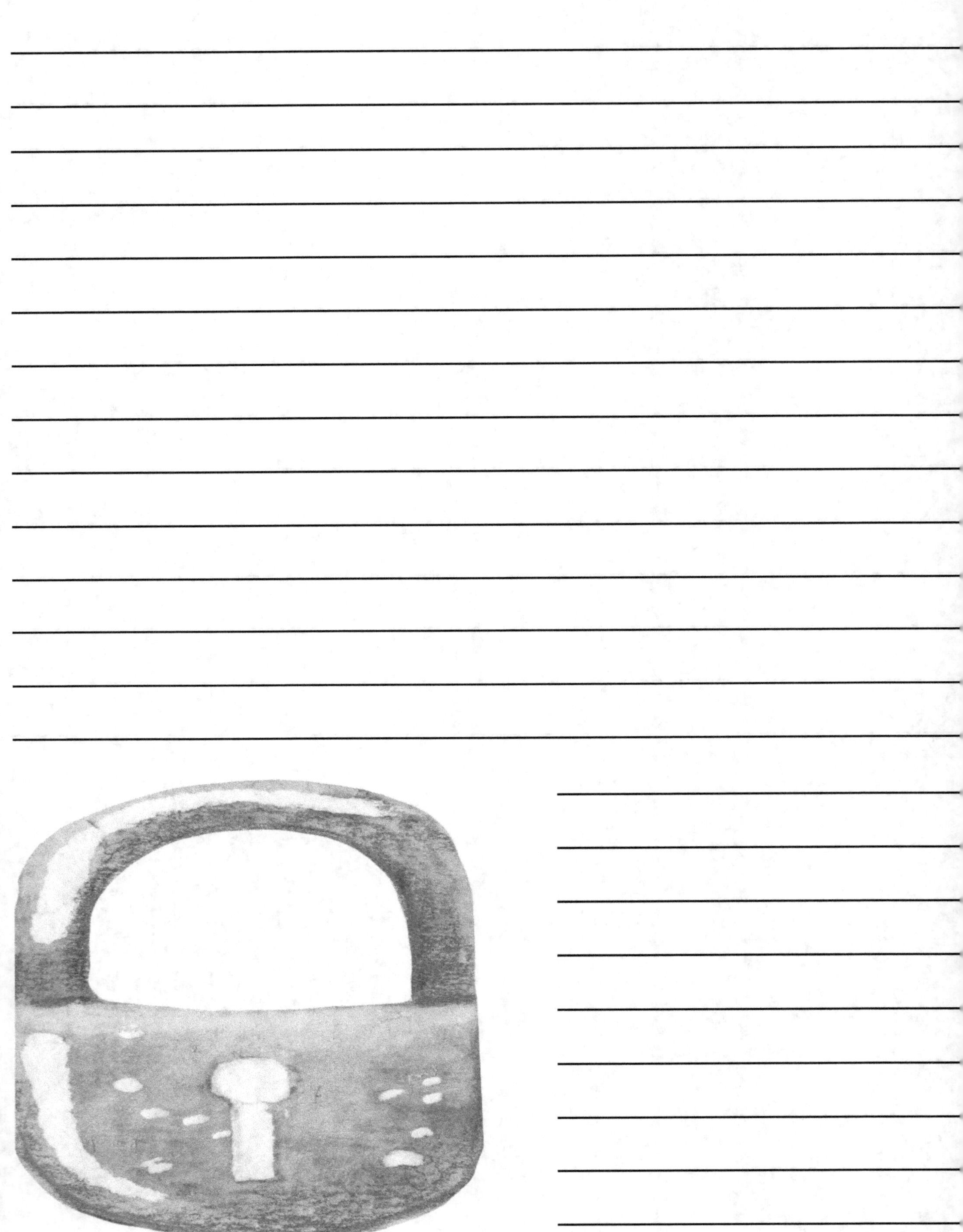

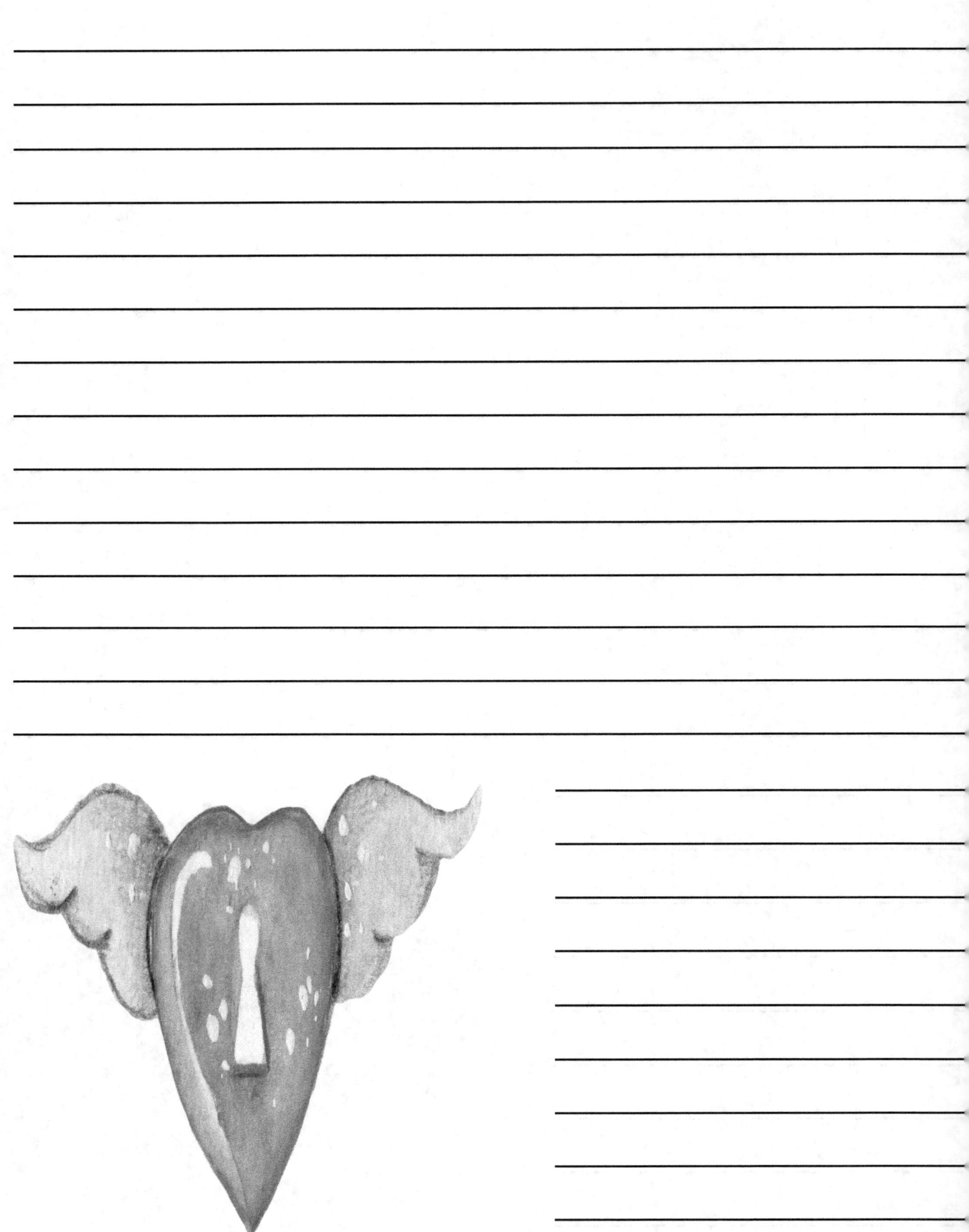

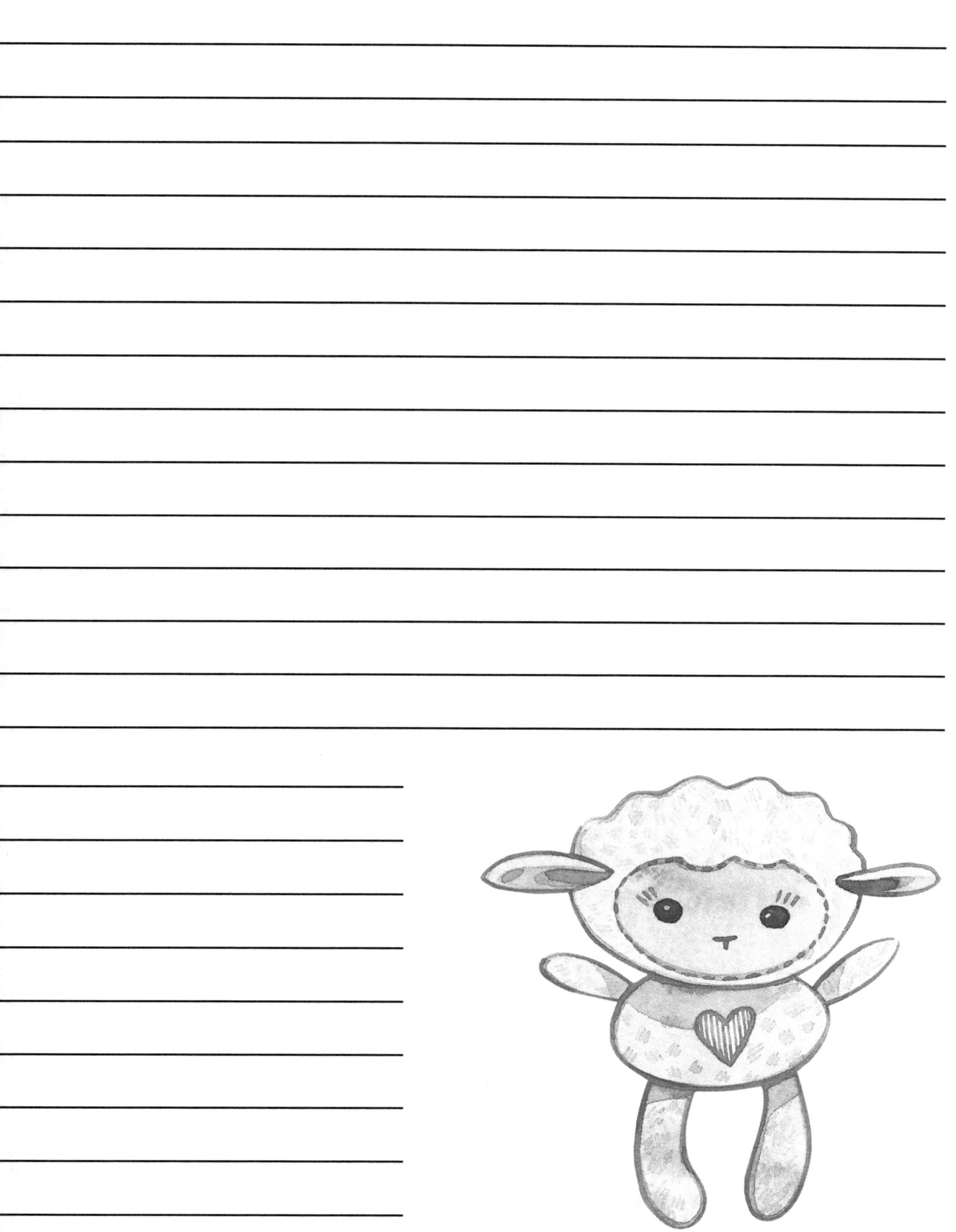

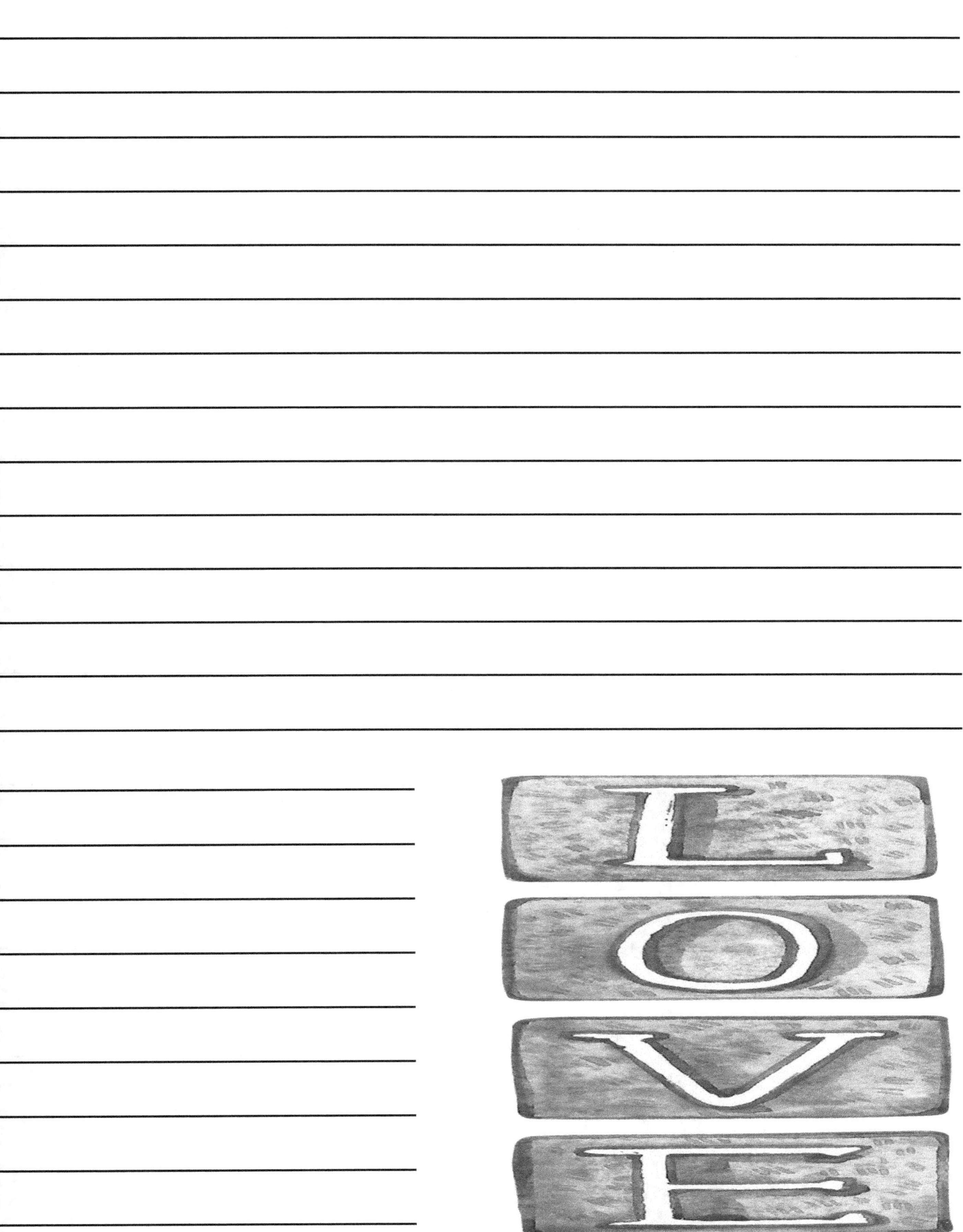
L
O
V
E

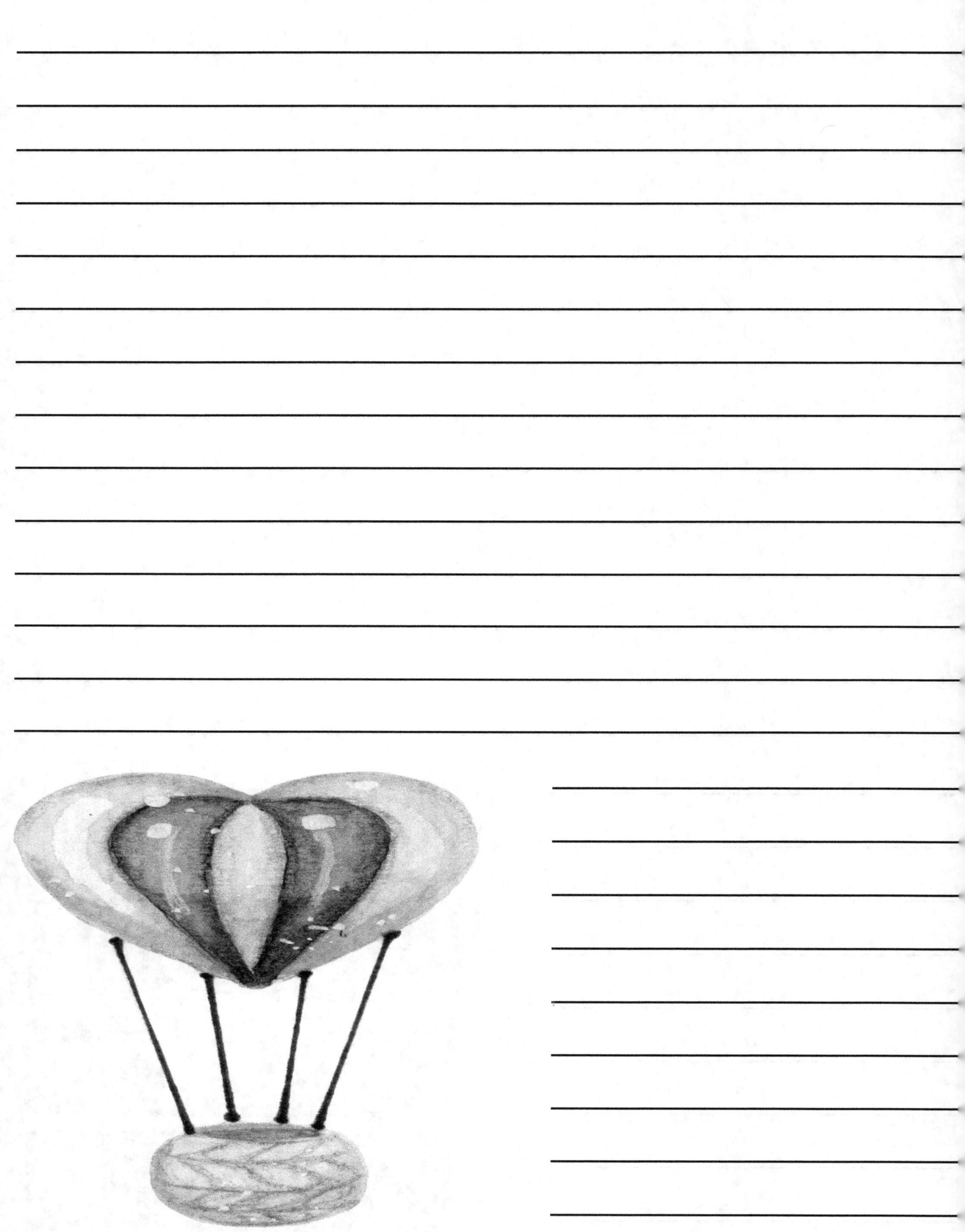

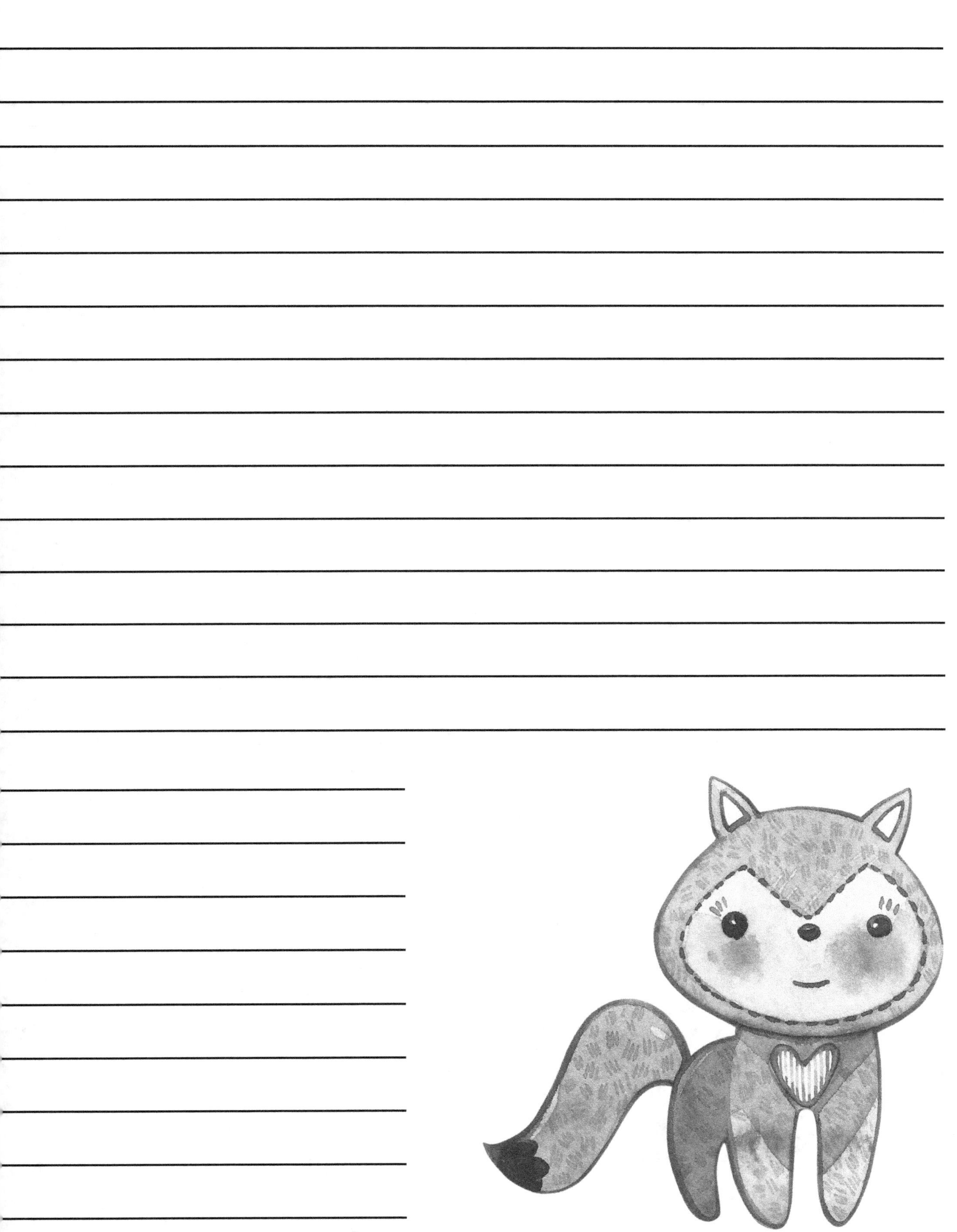

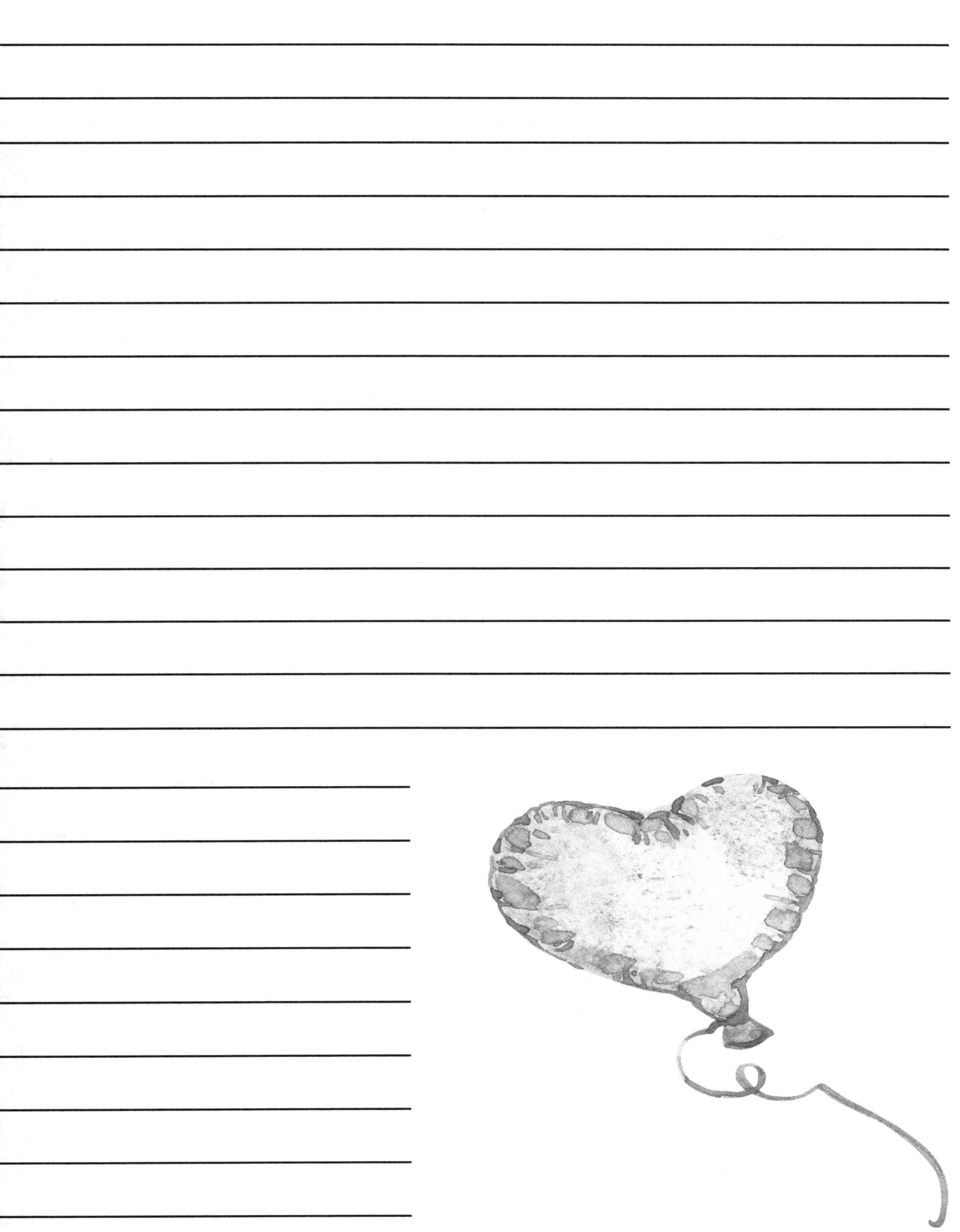

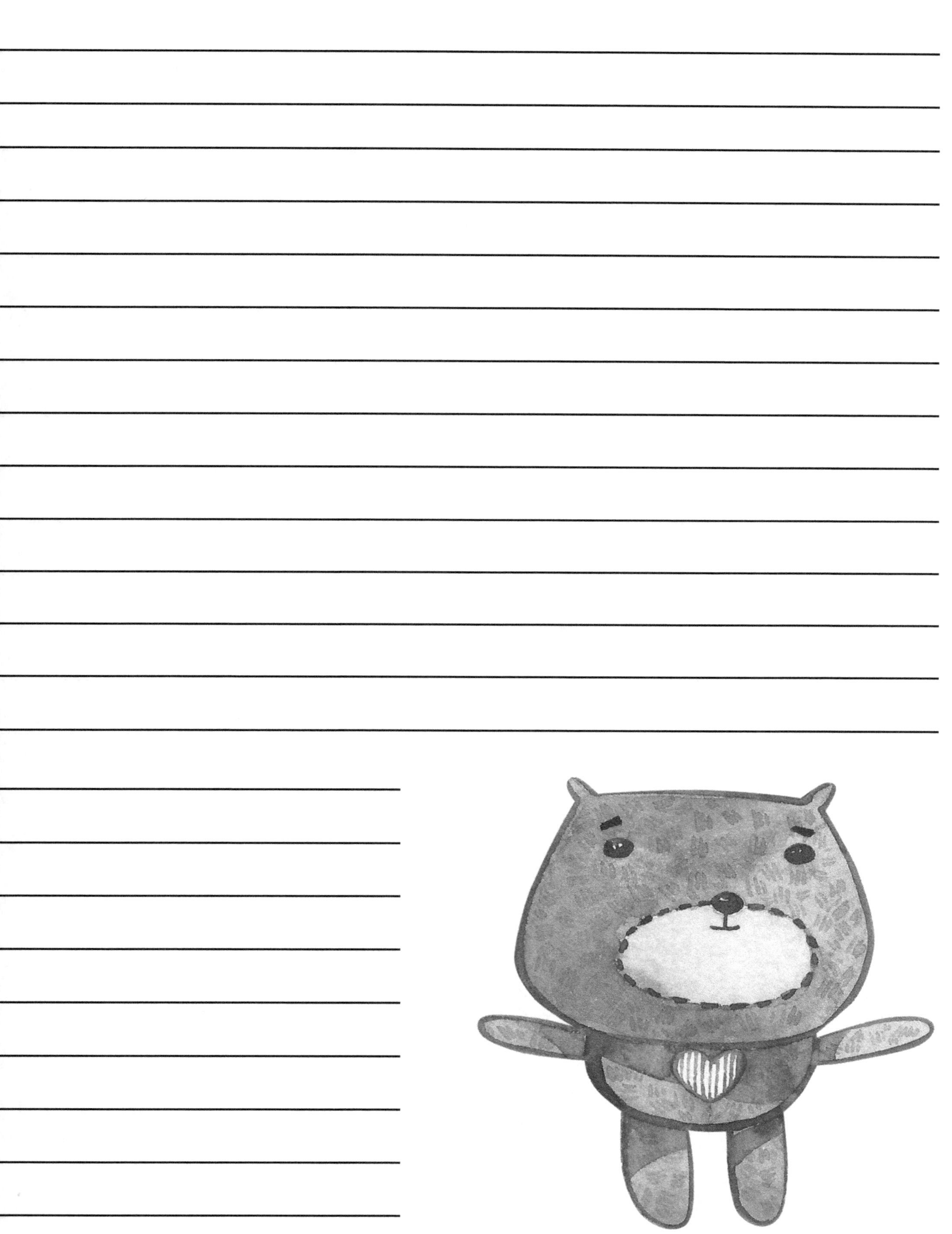

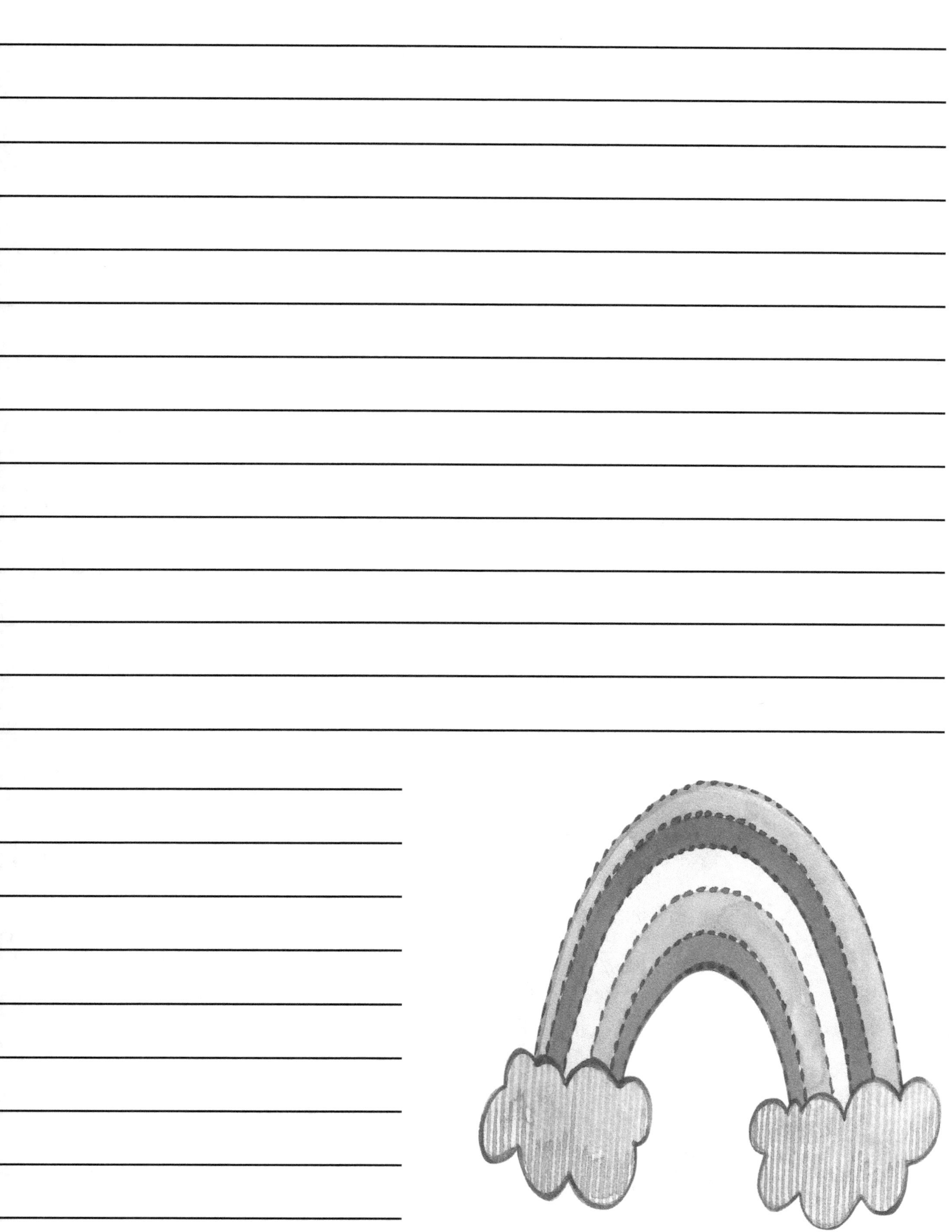

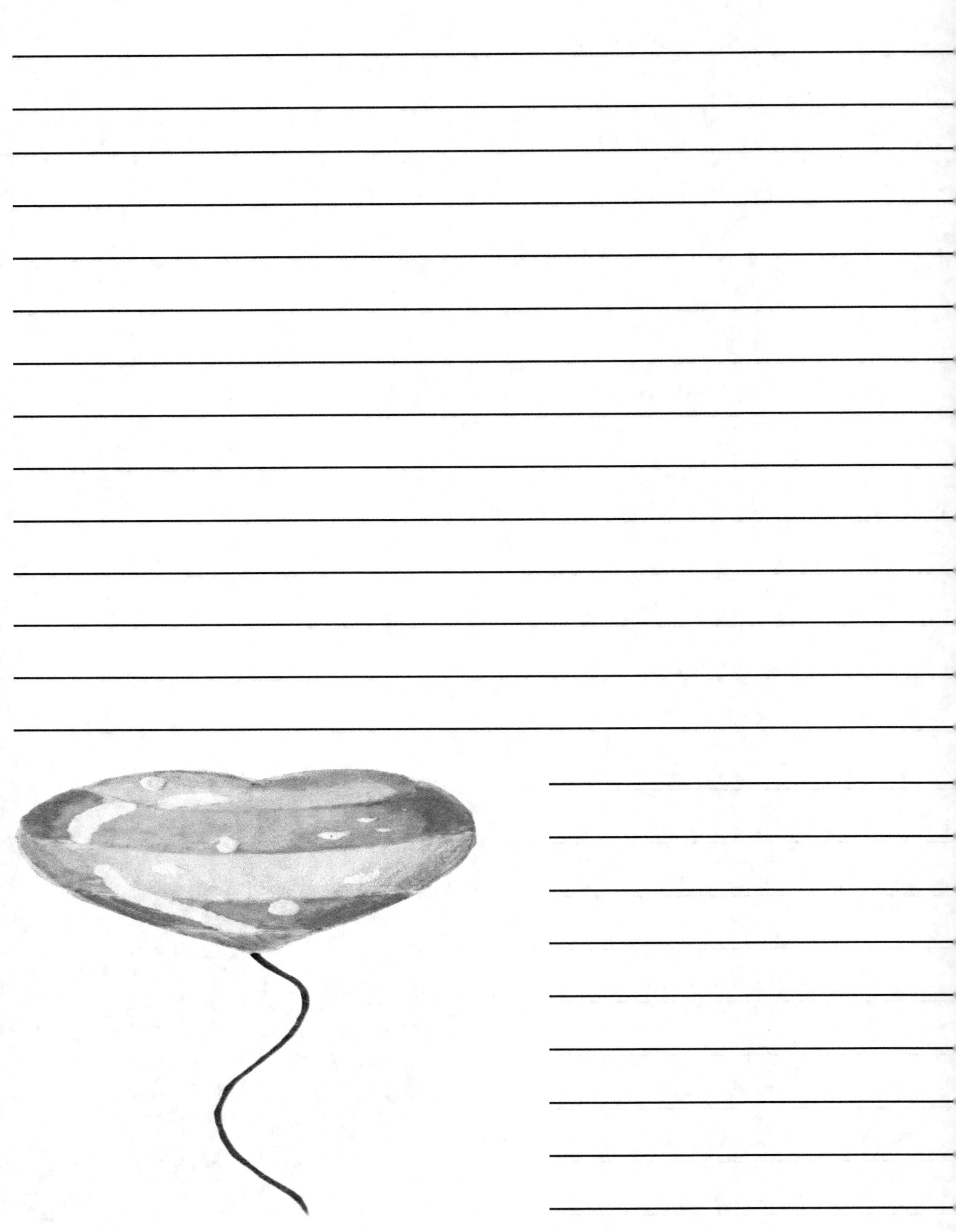

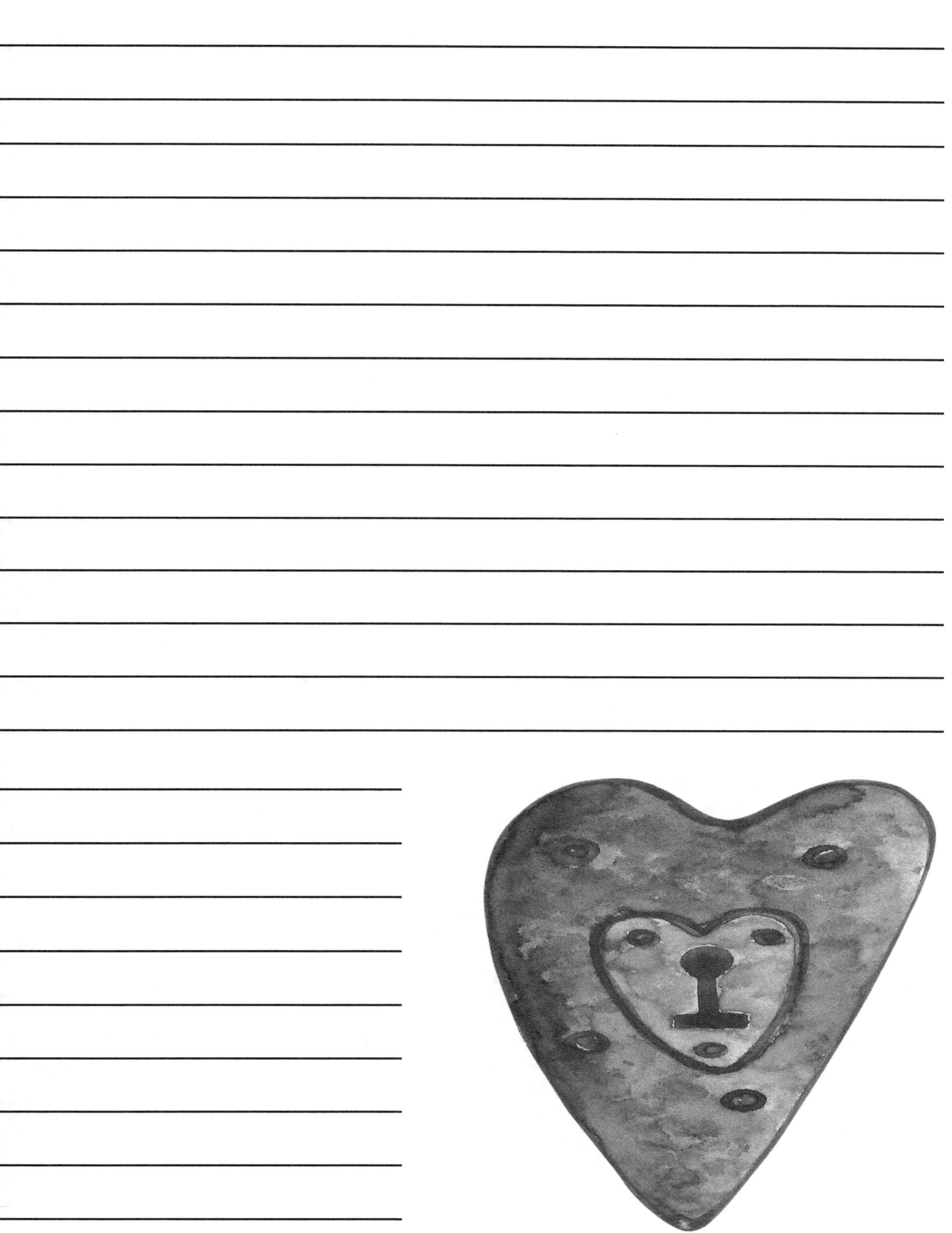

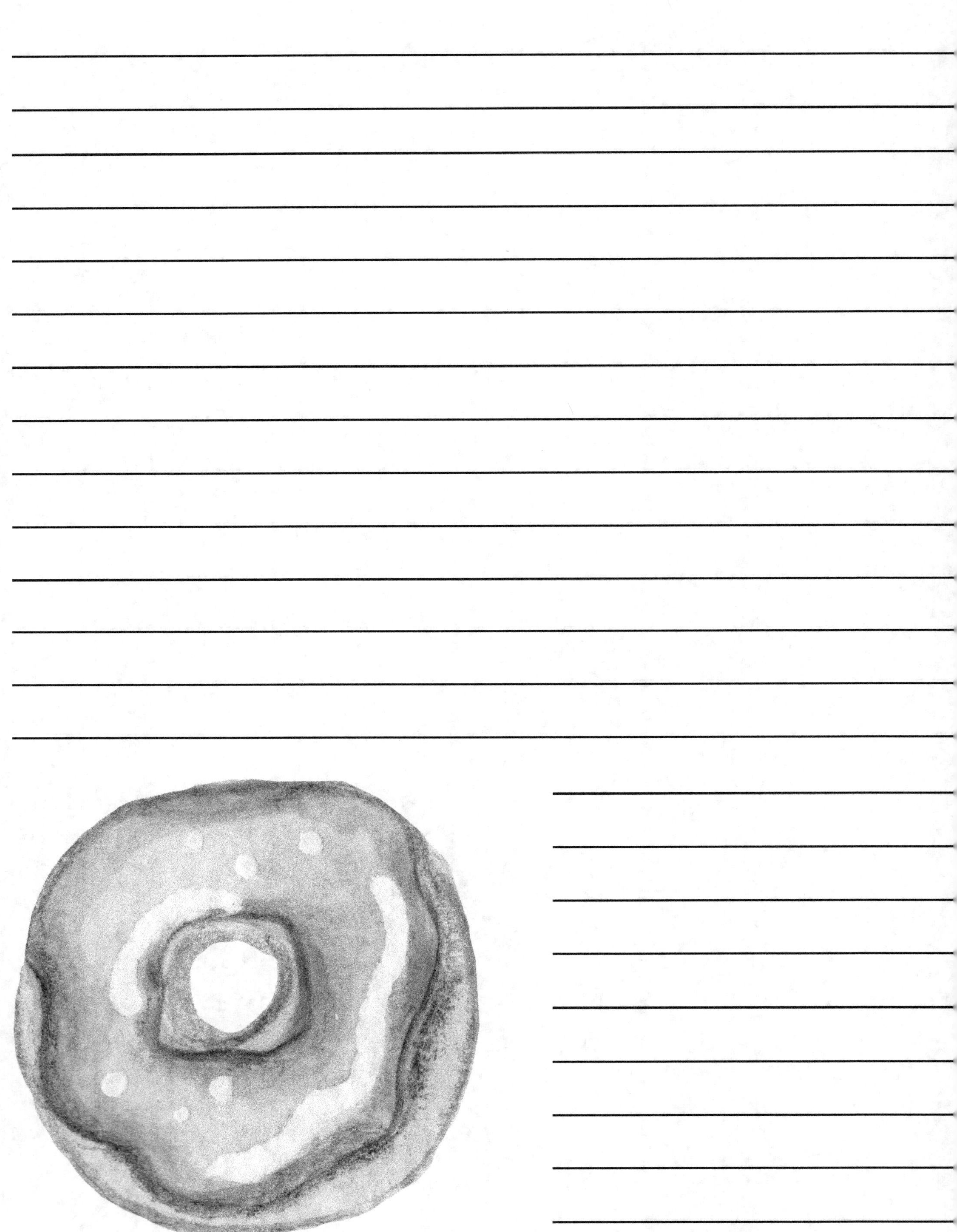

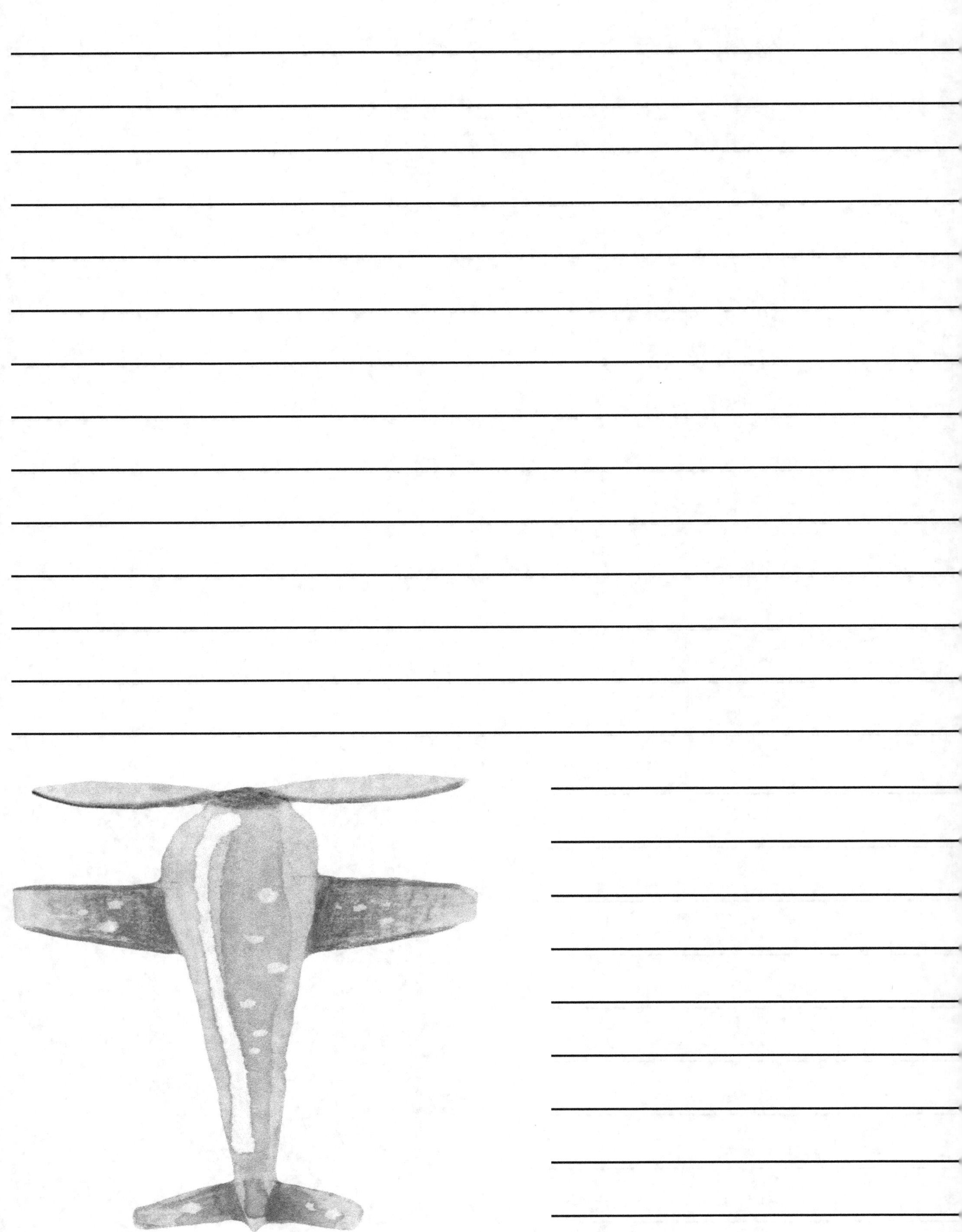

love

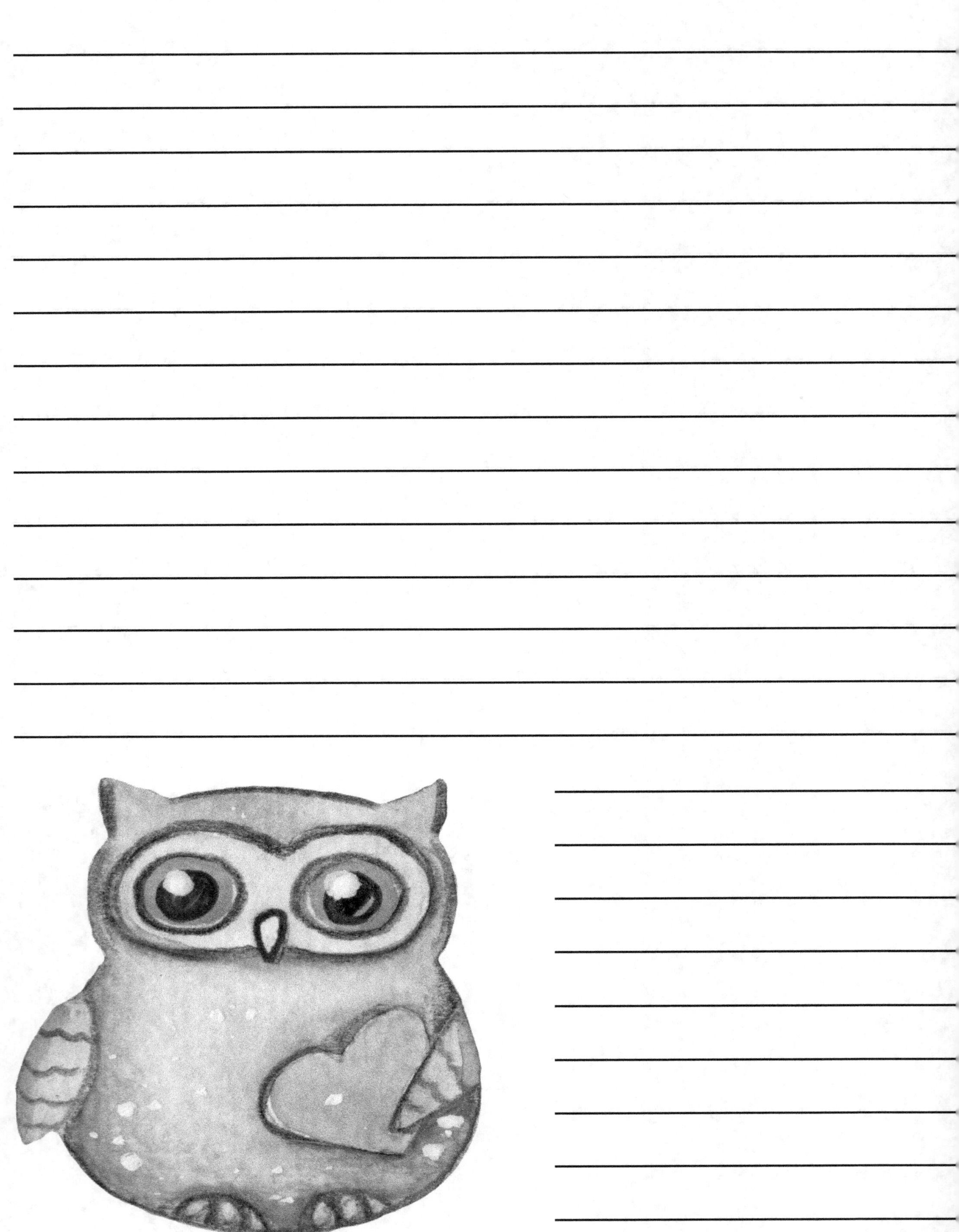

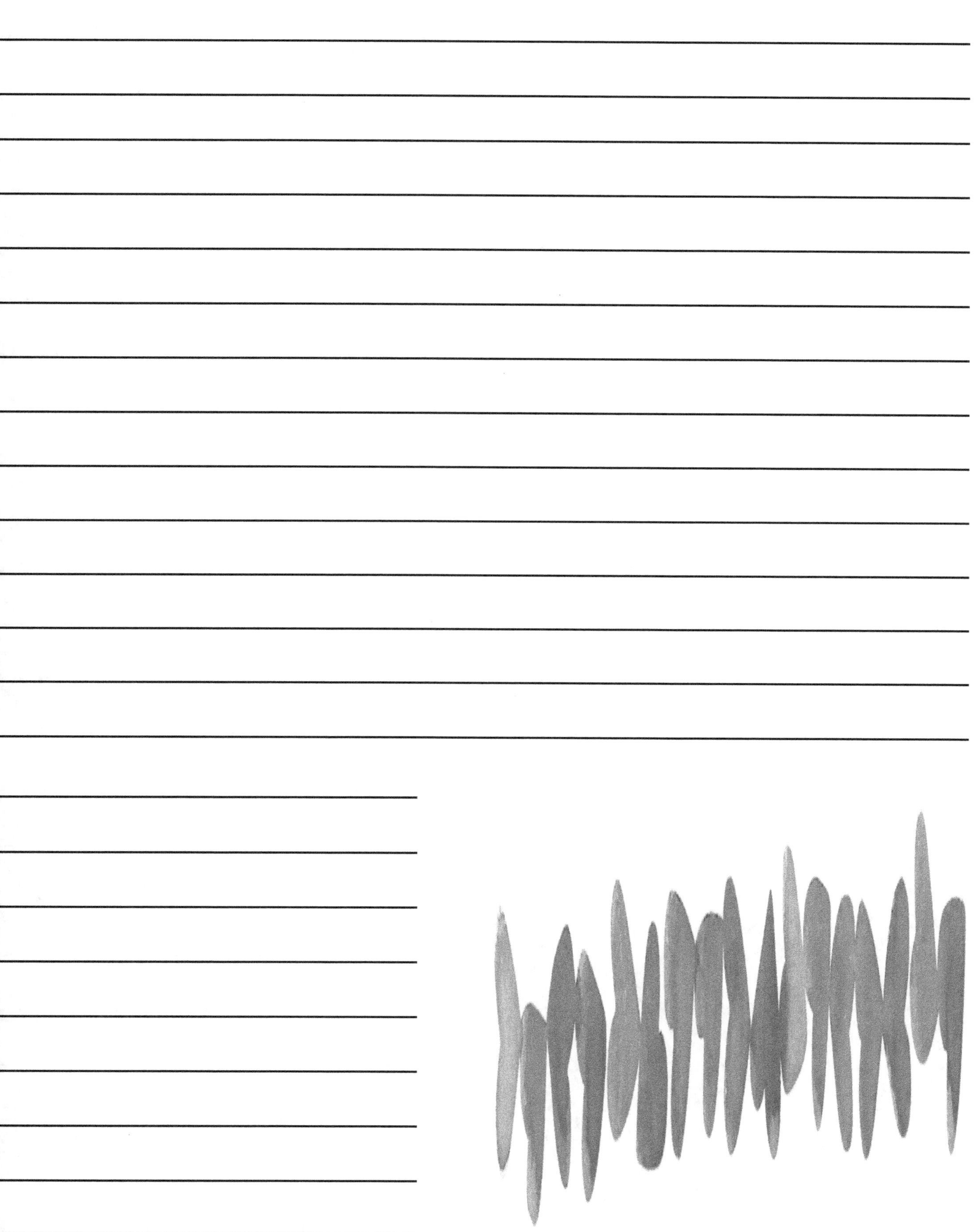

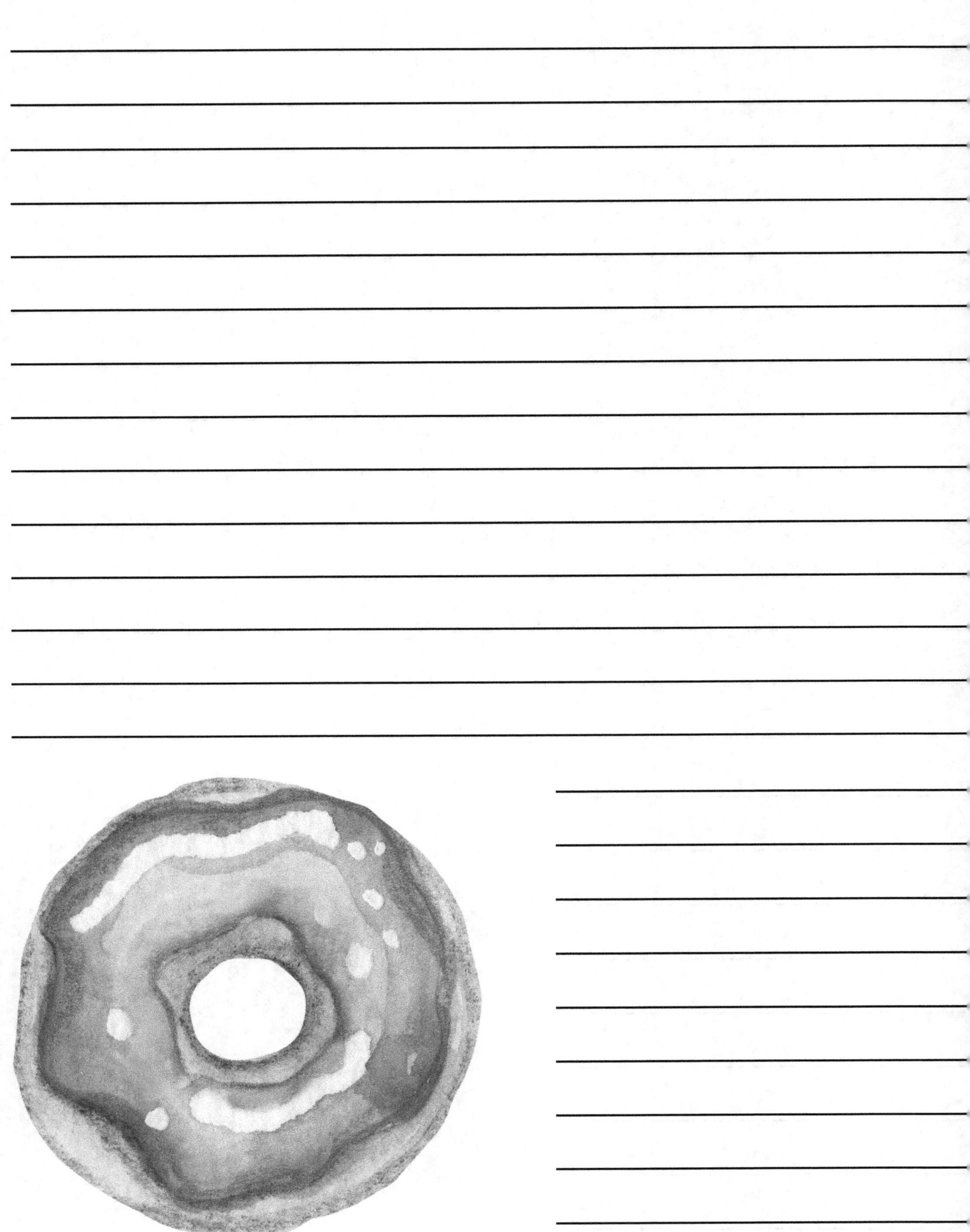

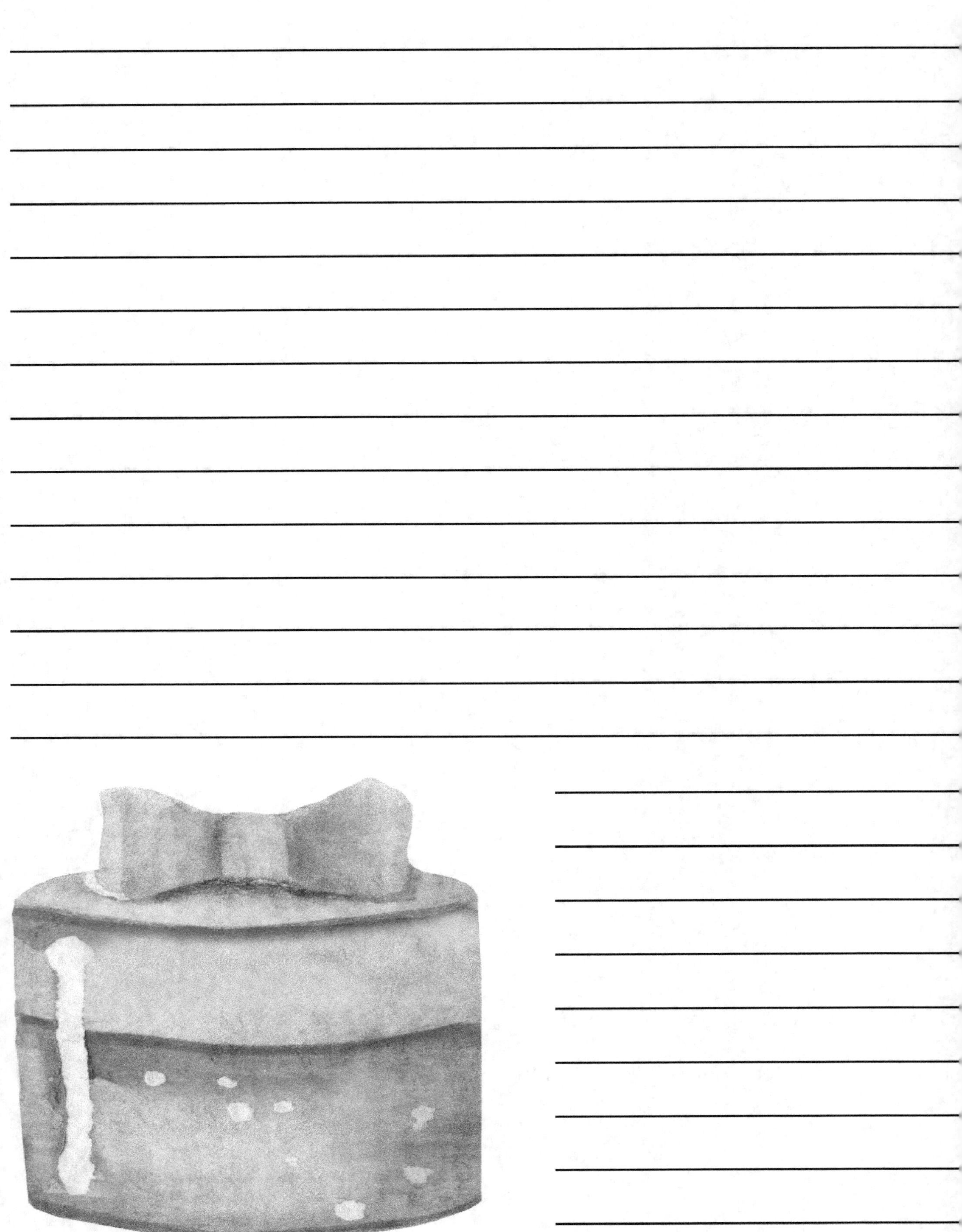

YAY

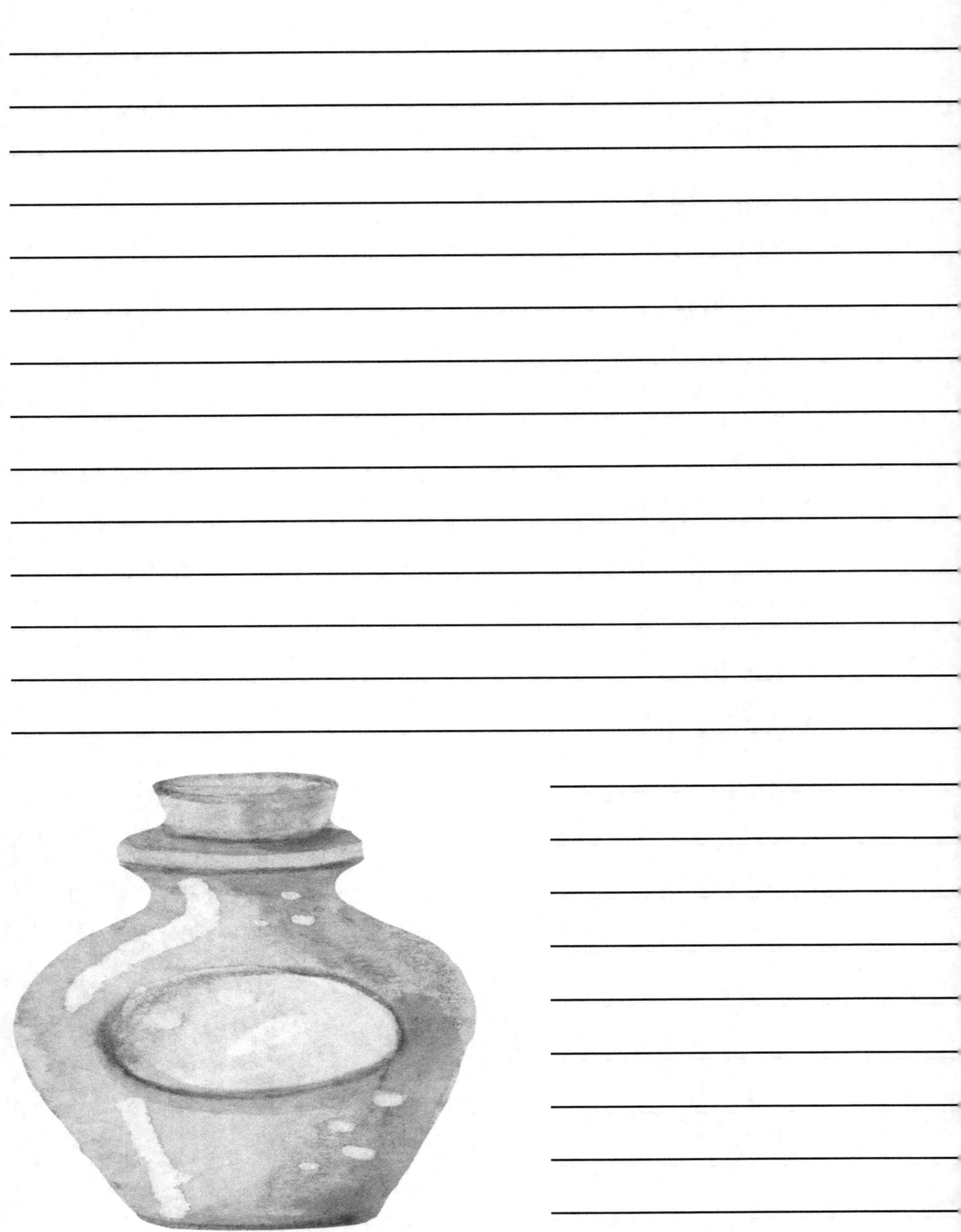

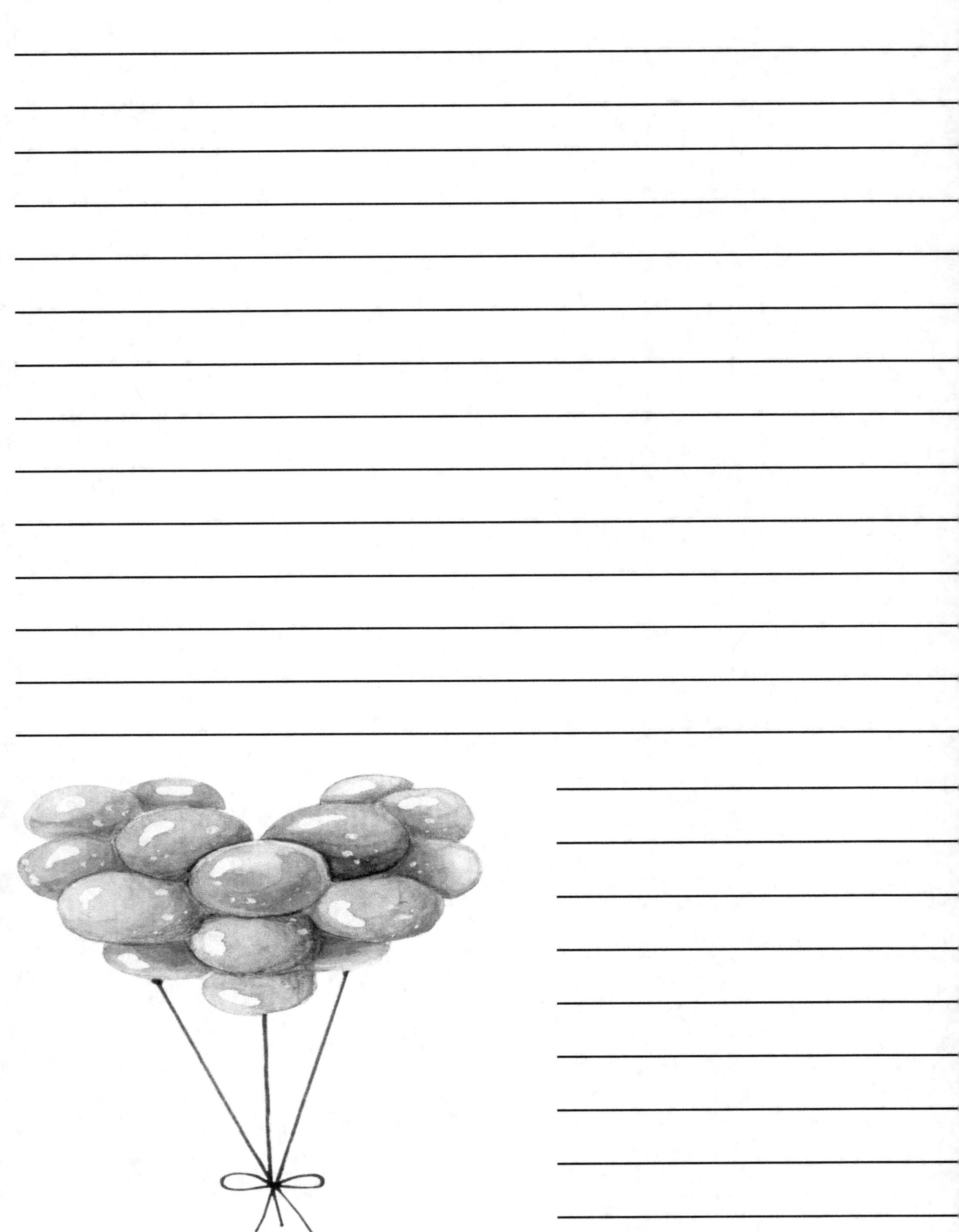

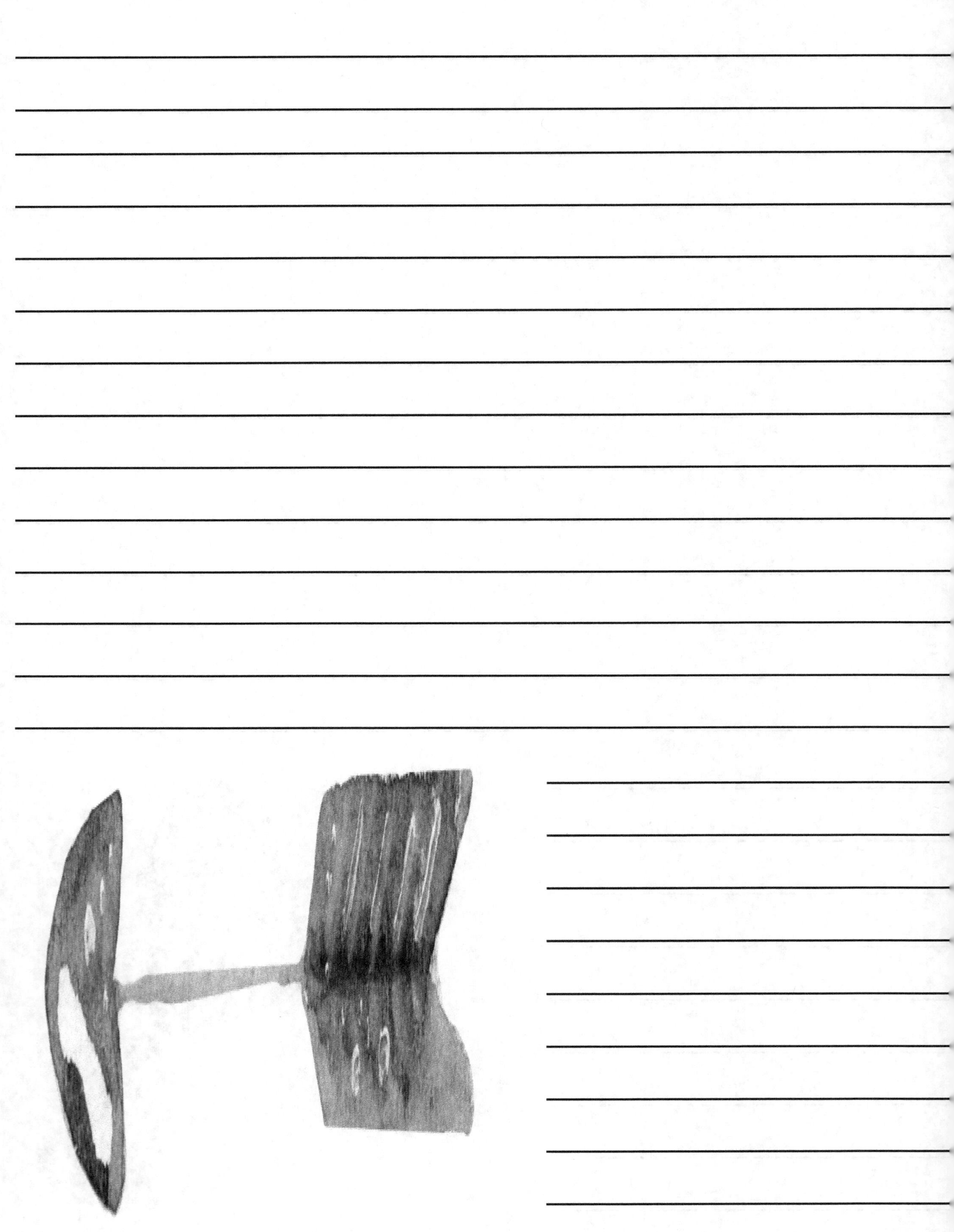

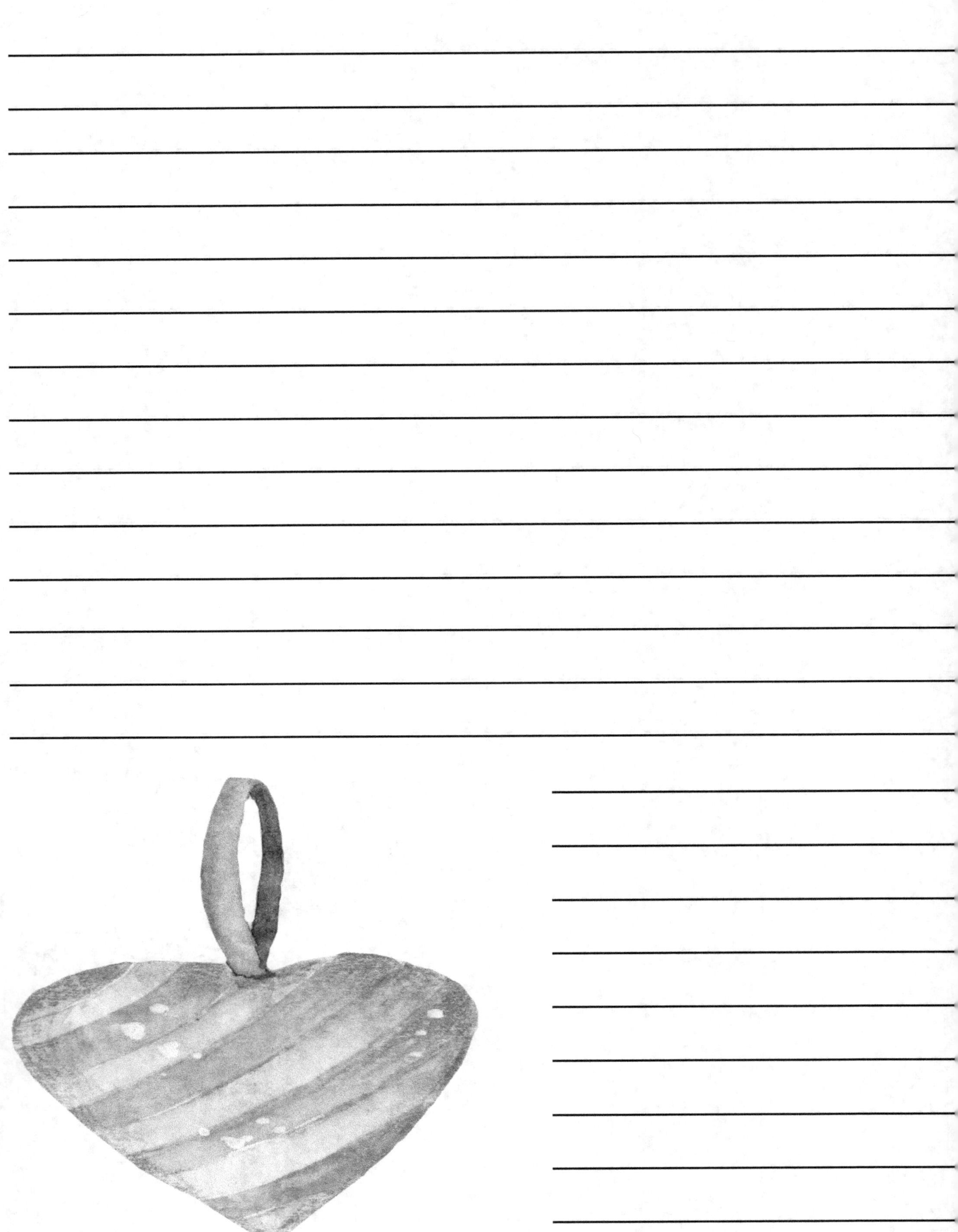

you
+
me
=
love

believe
IN
Love

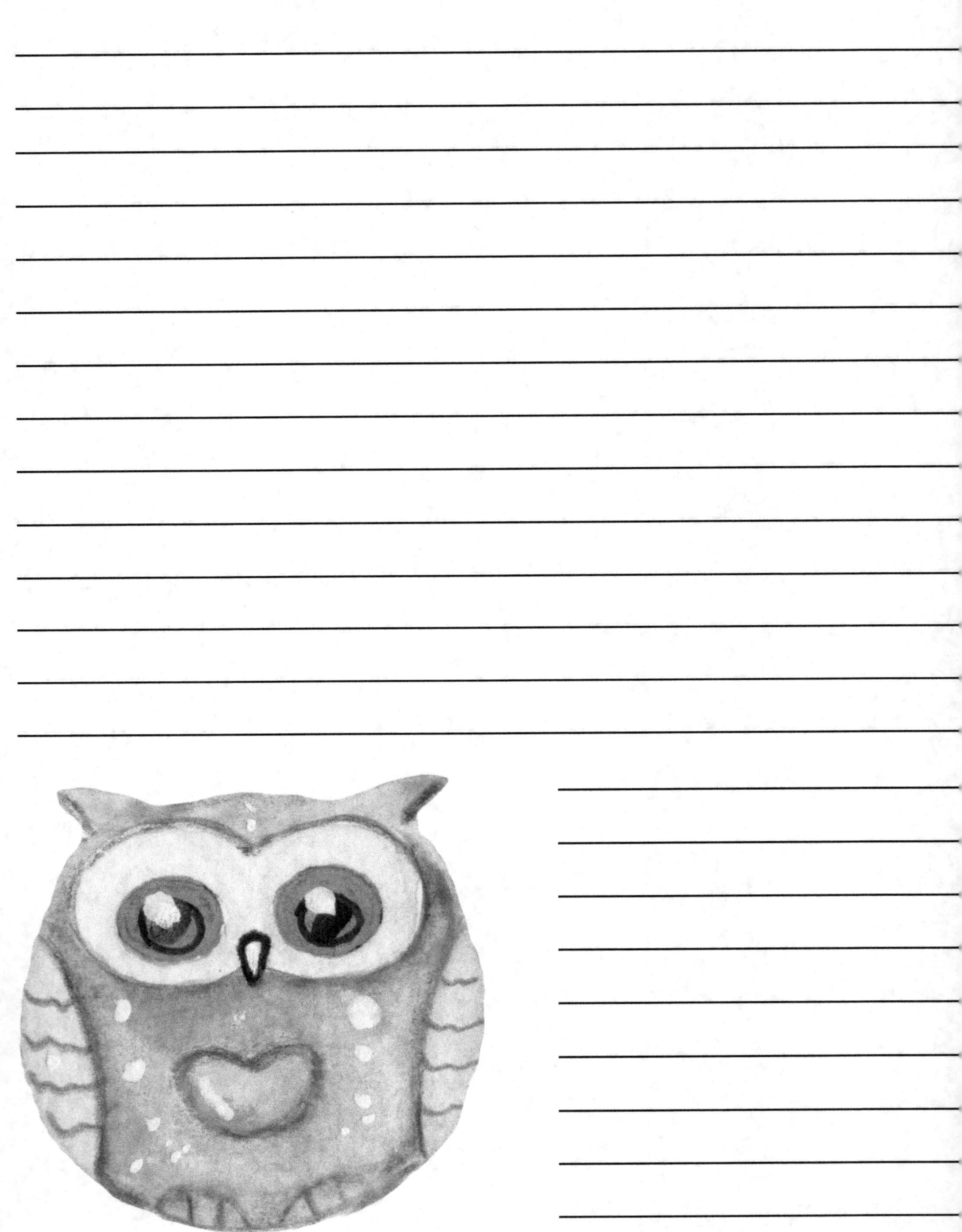

love

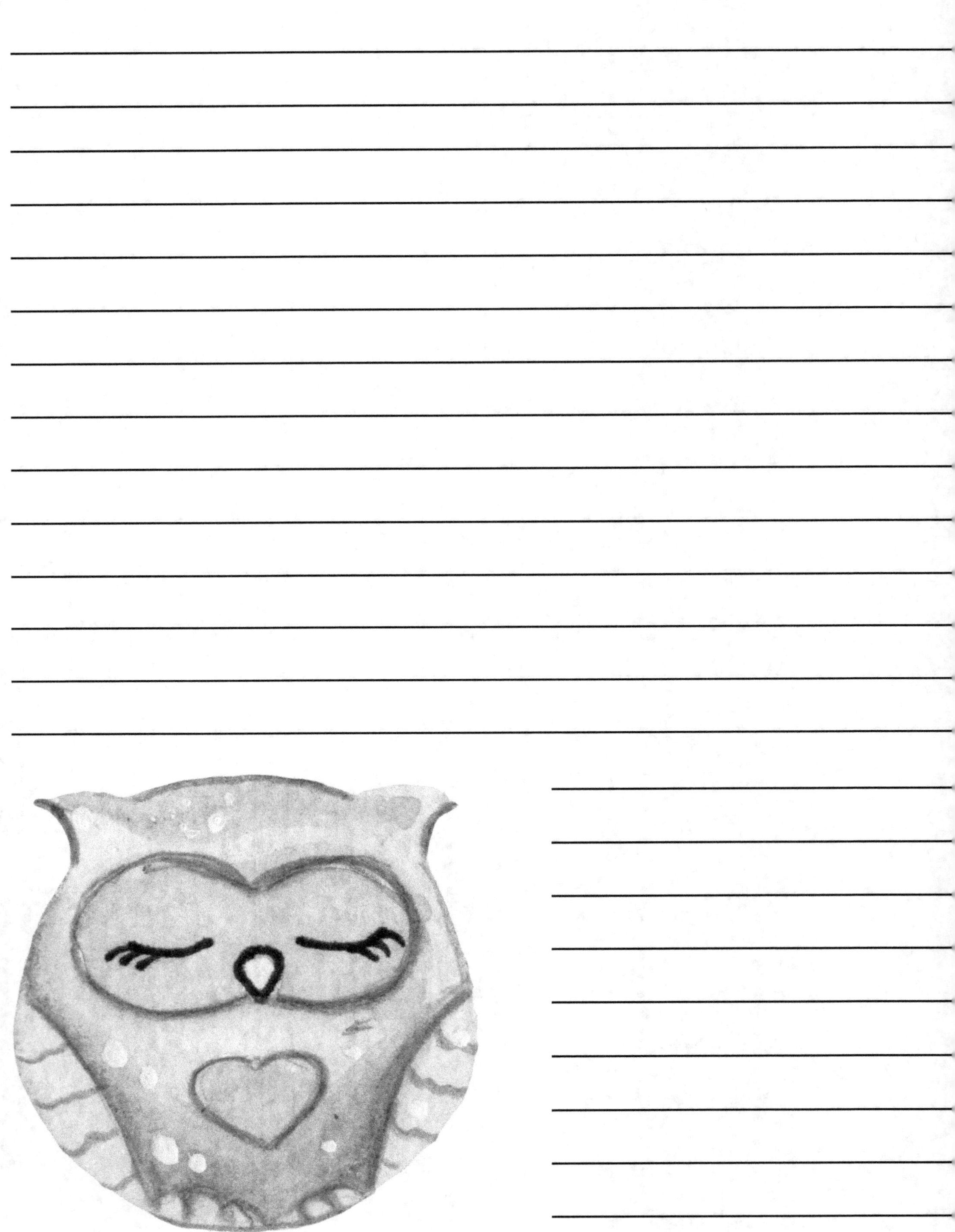

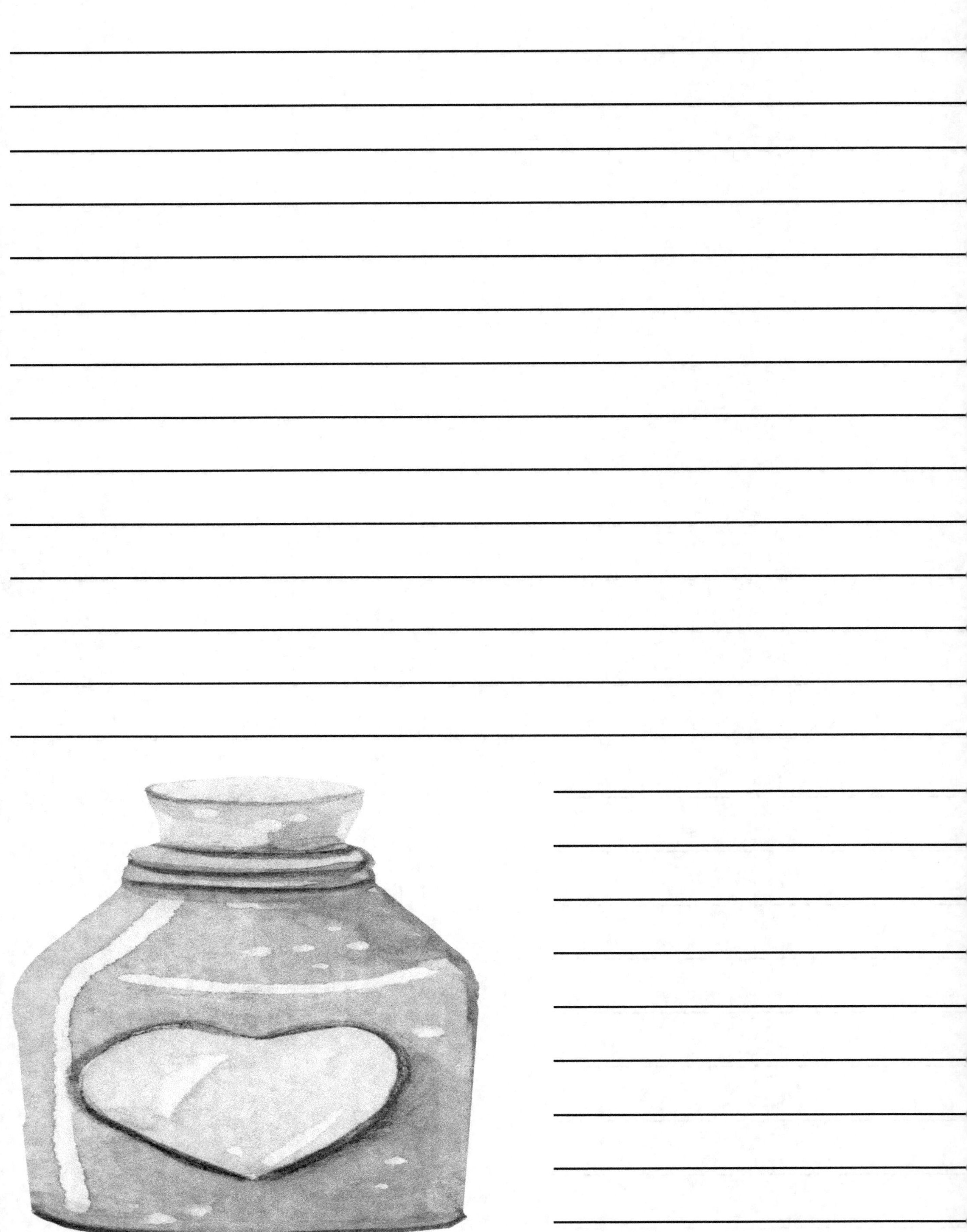

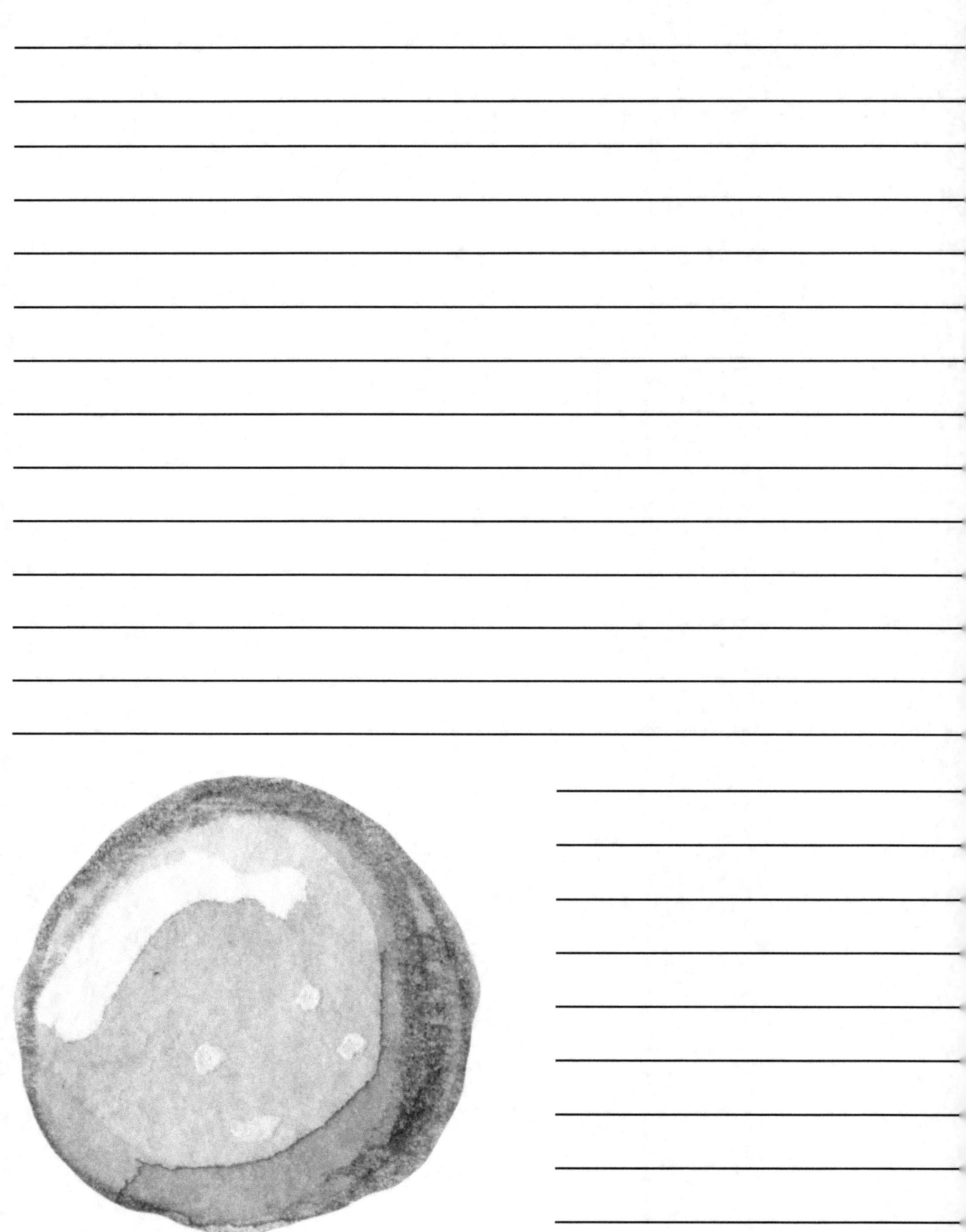

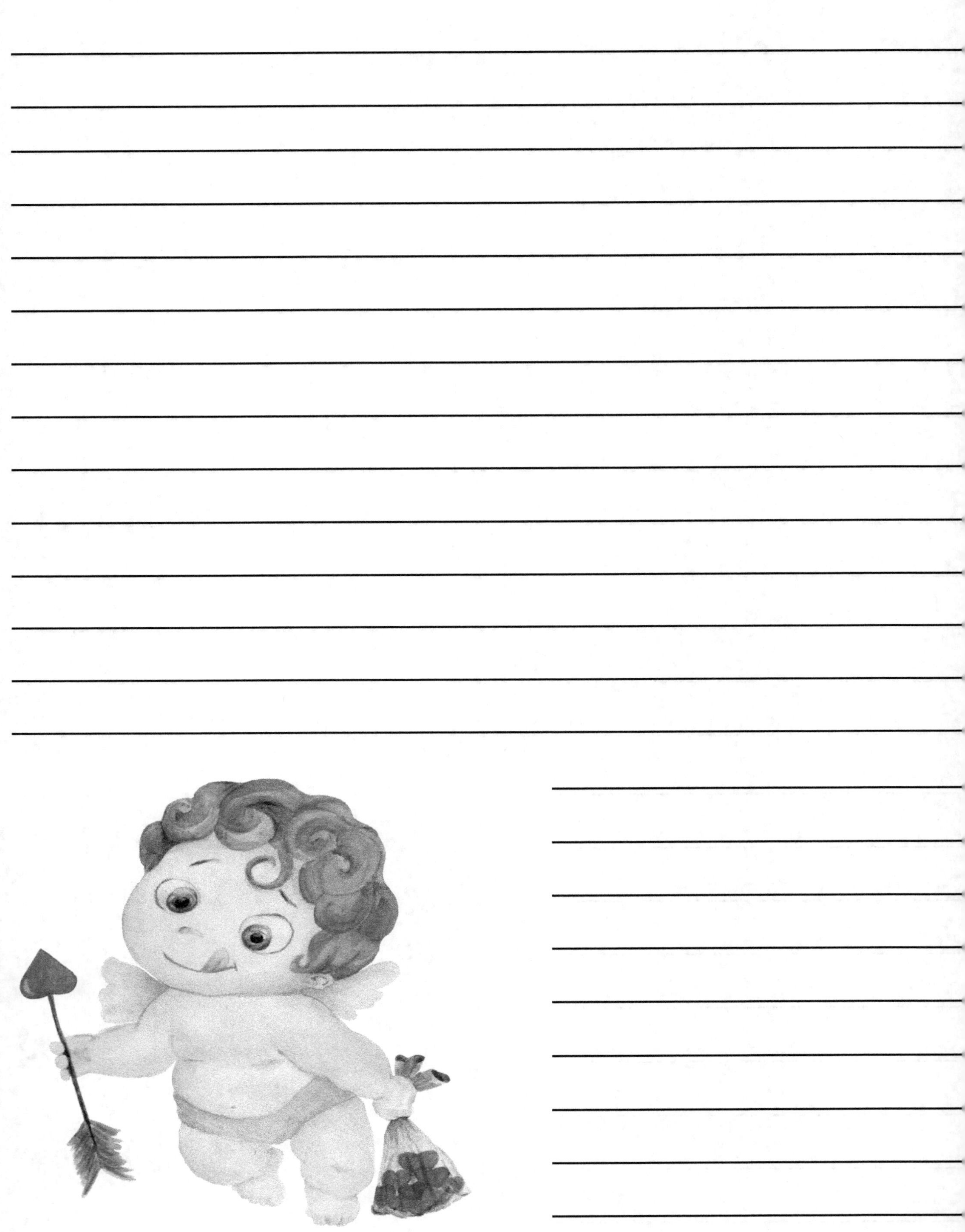

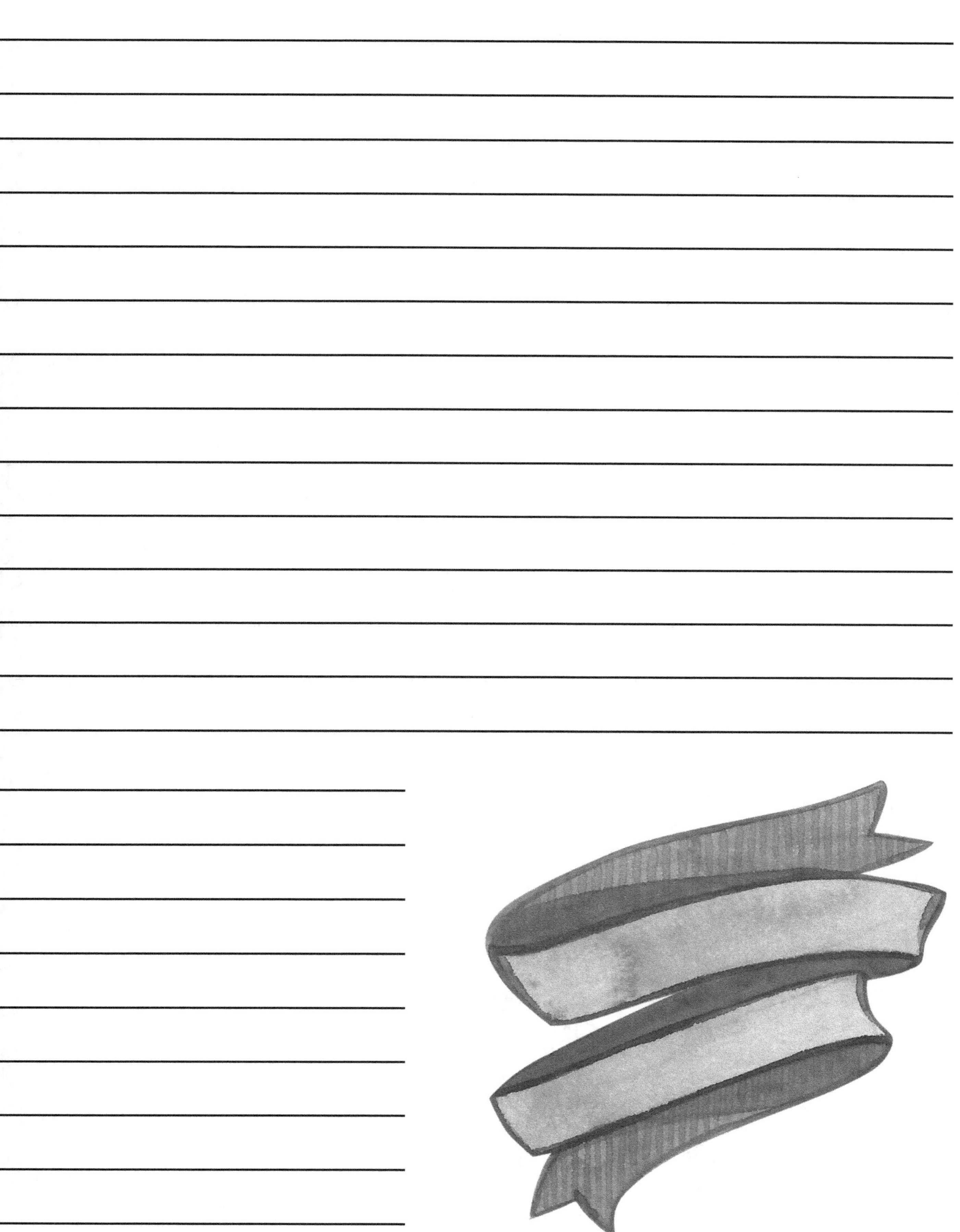

i love you

love you

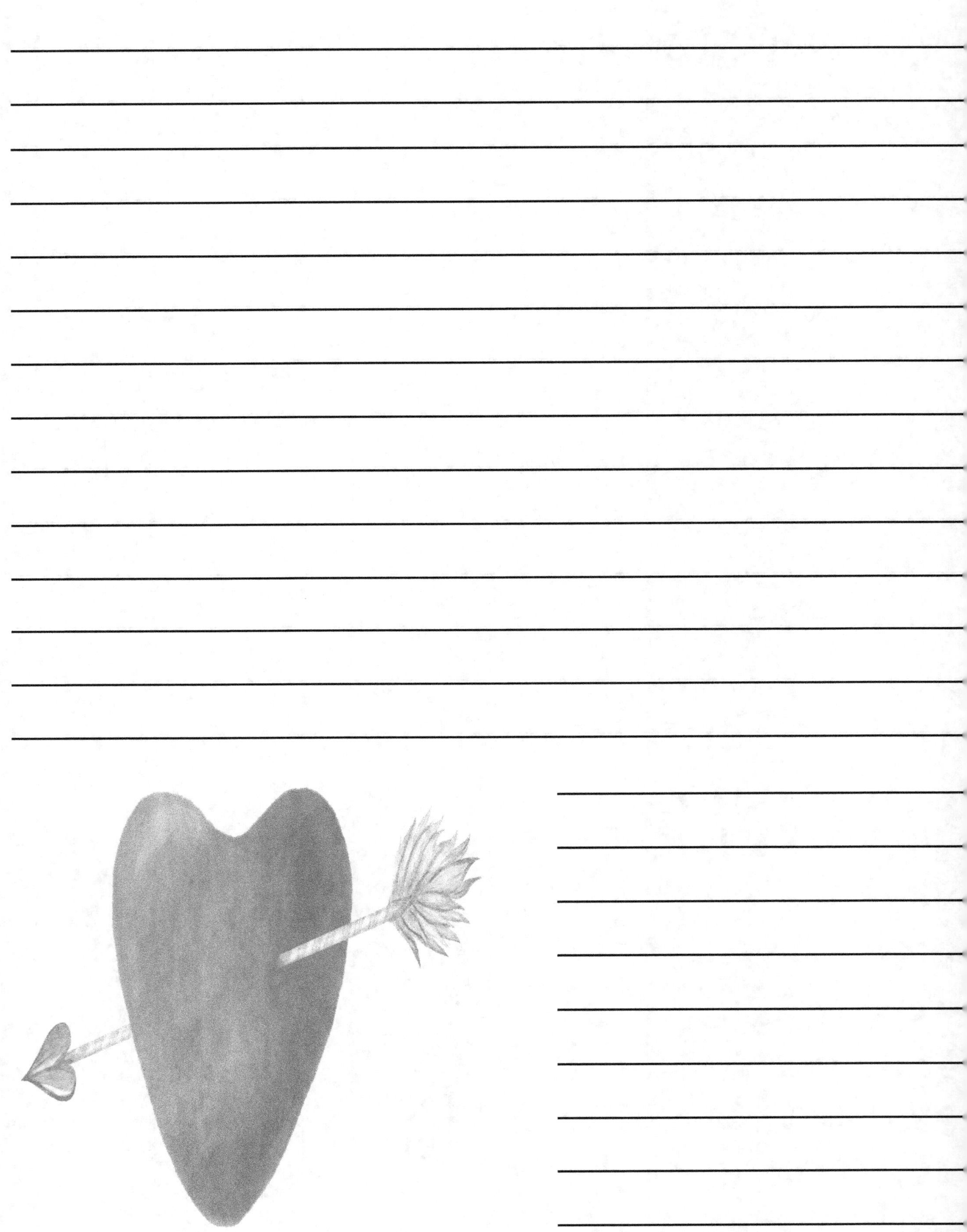

Love

LOVE

LOVE

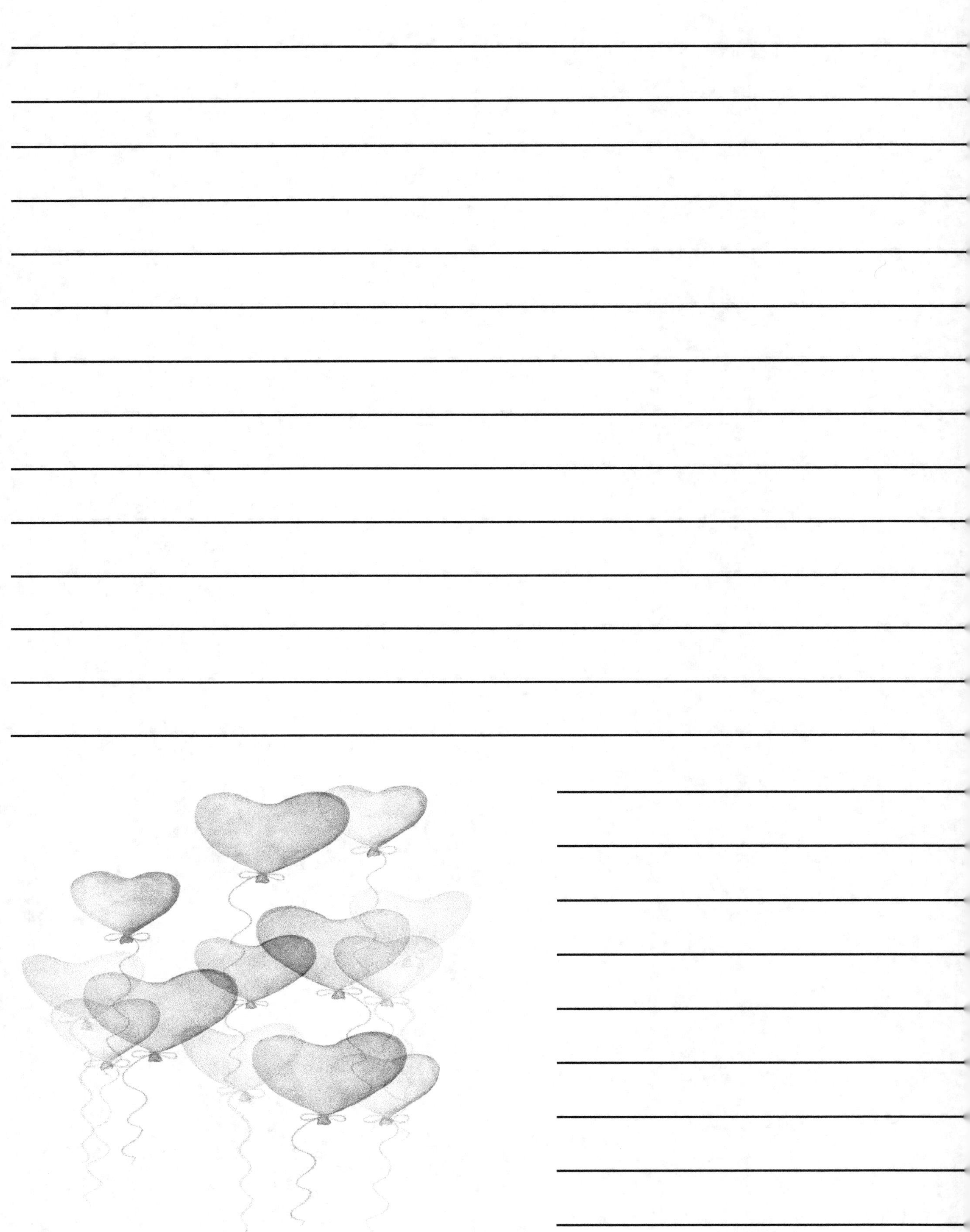

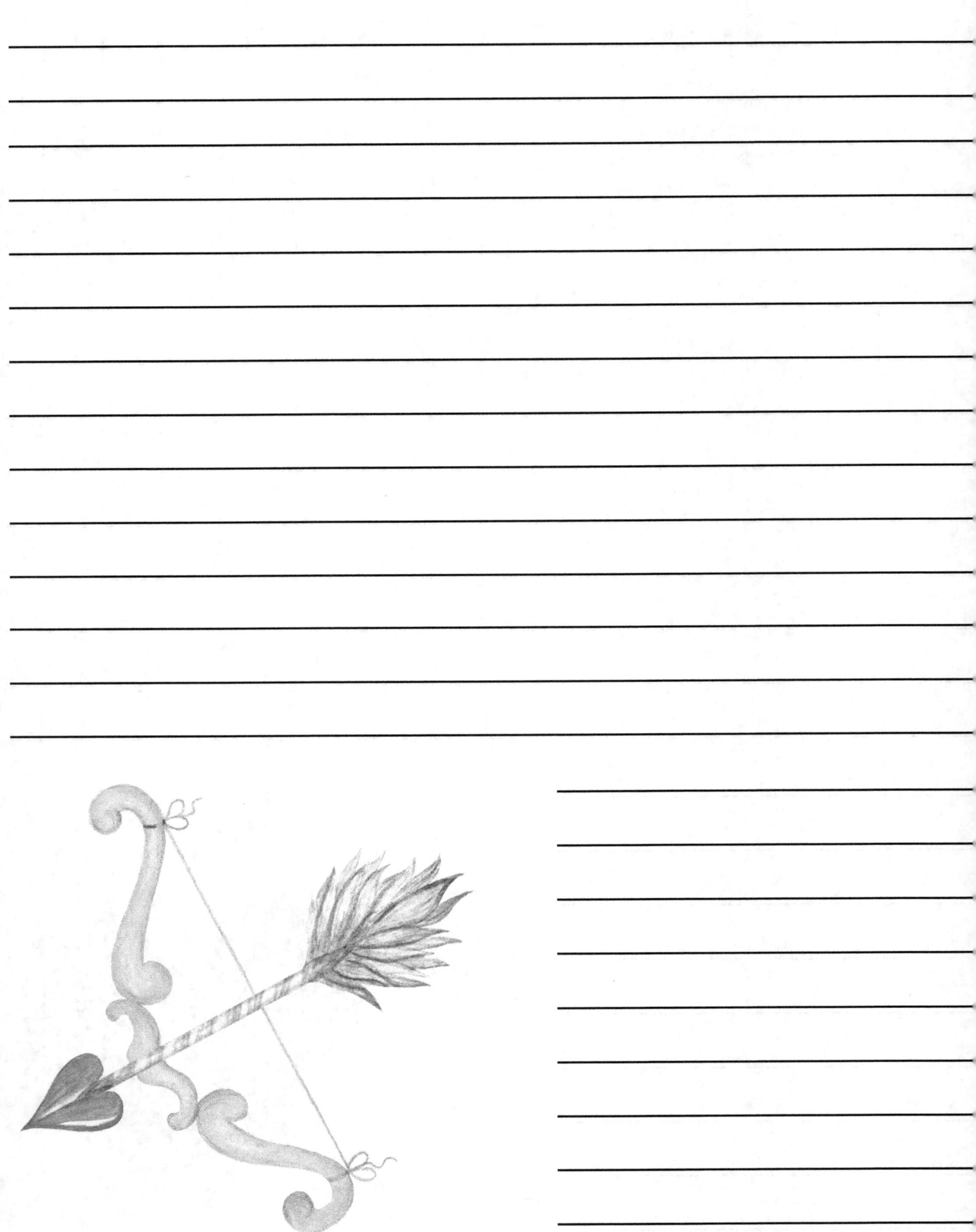

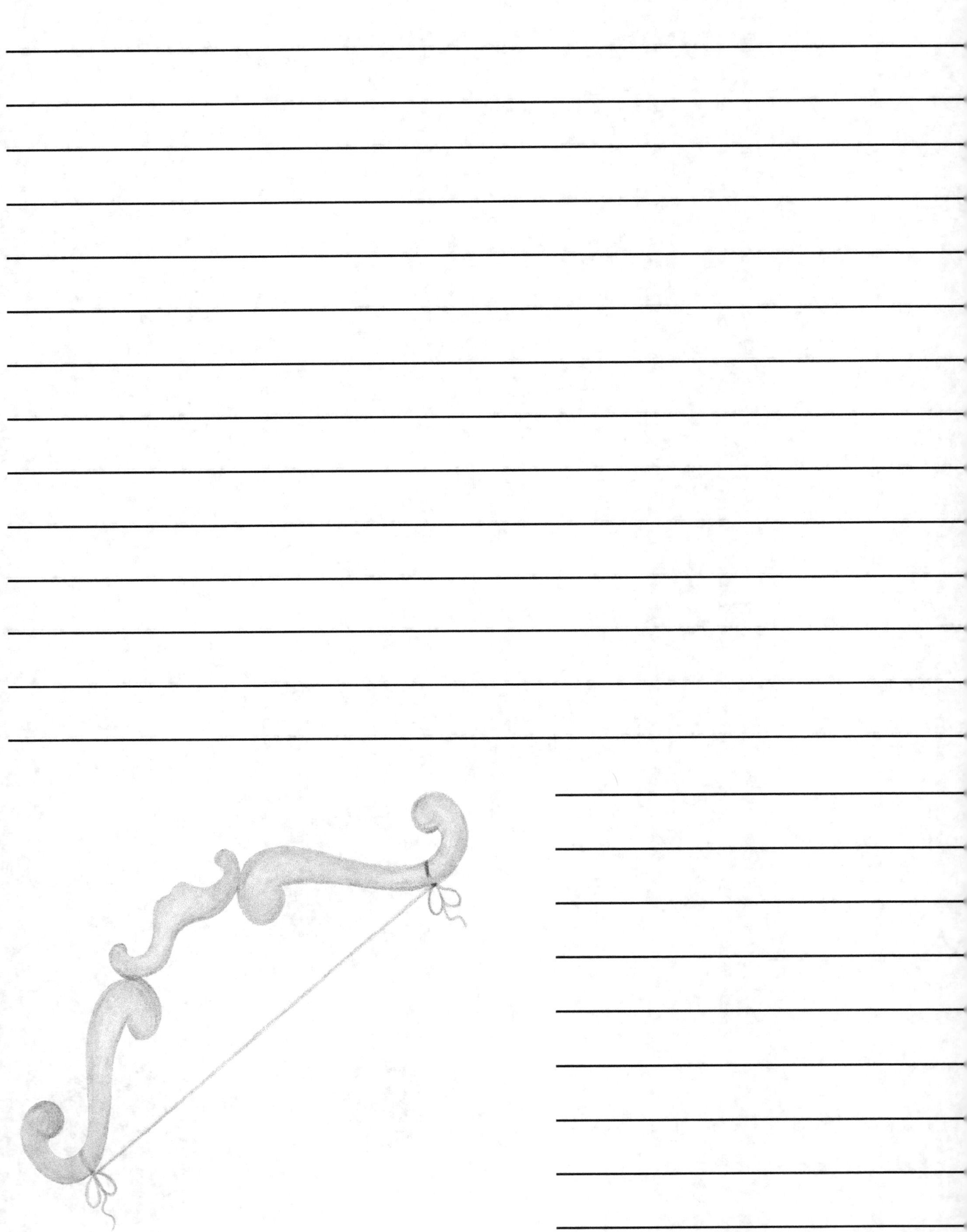

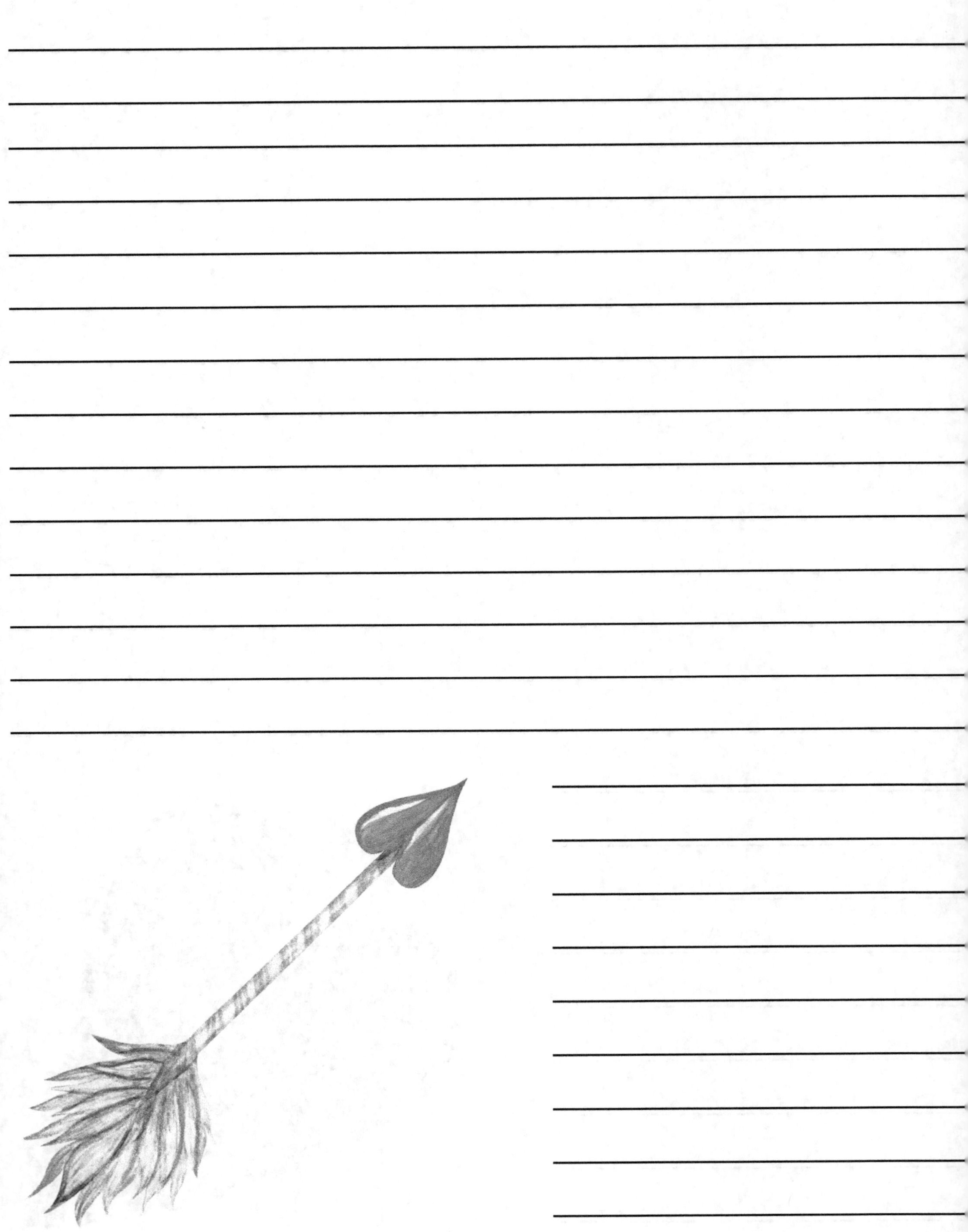

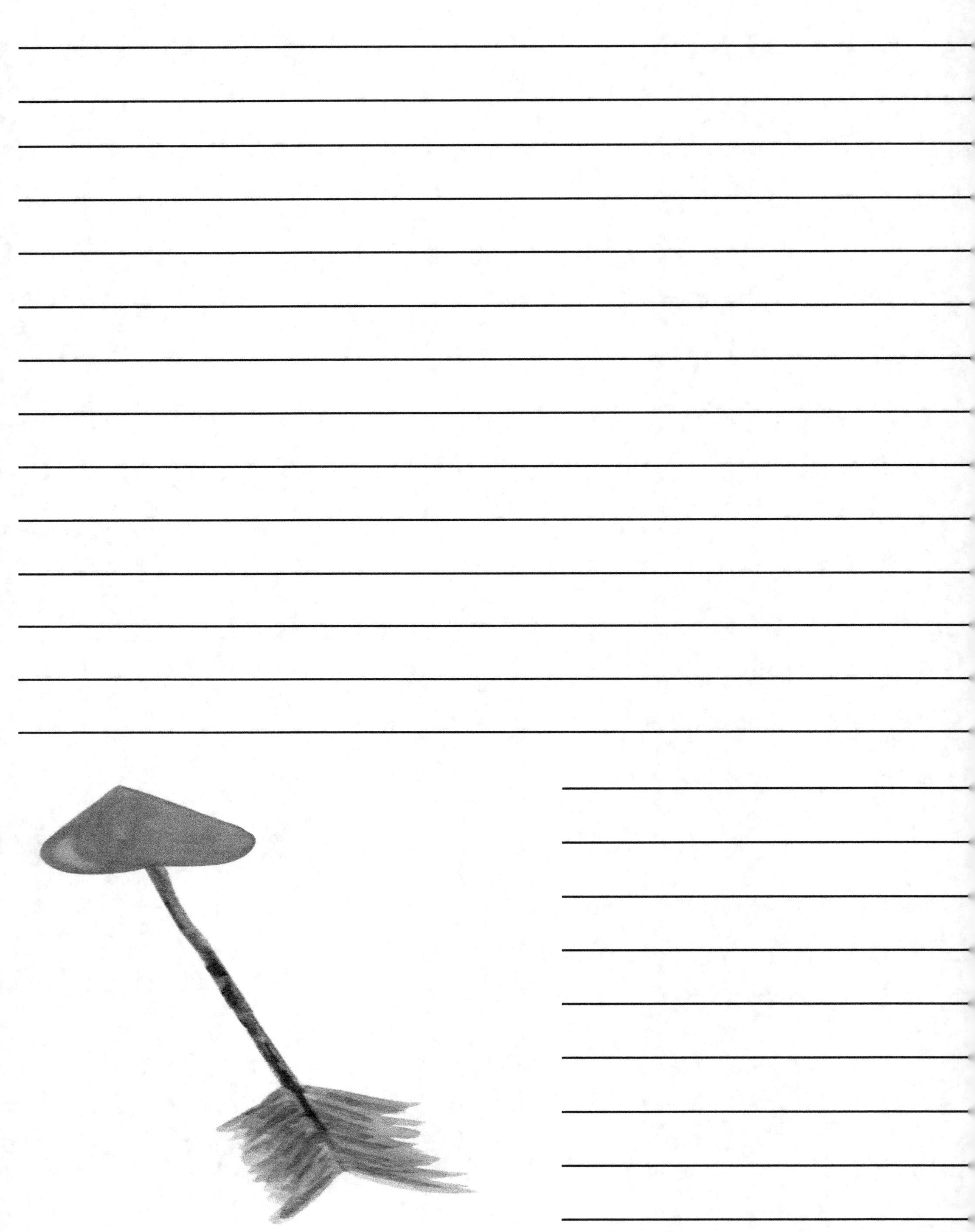

you are loved

love is all you need

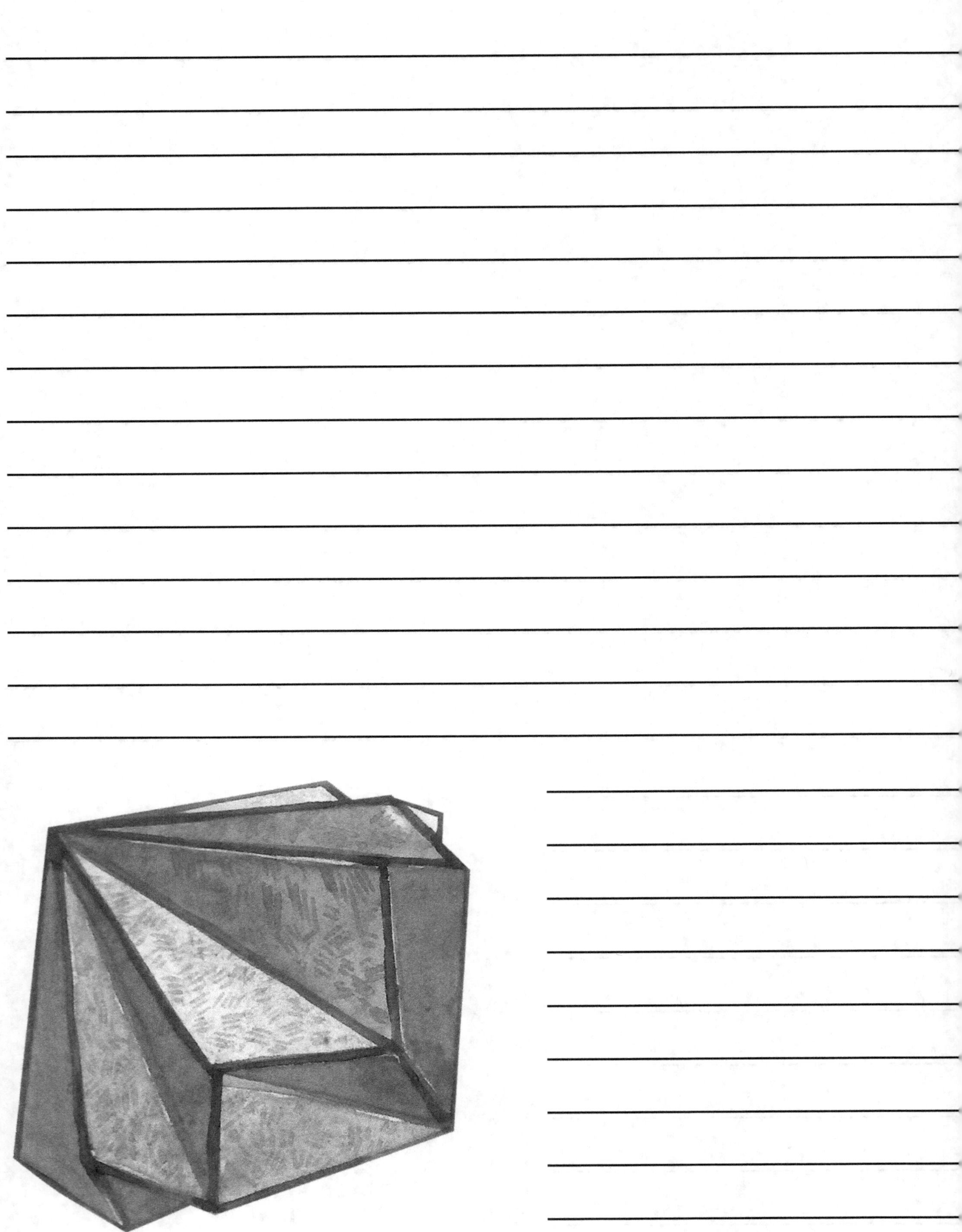

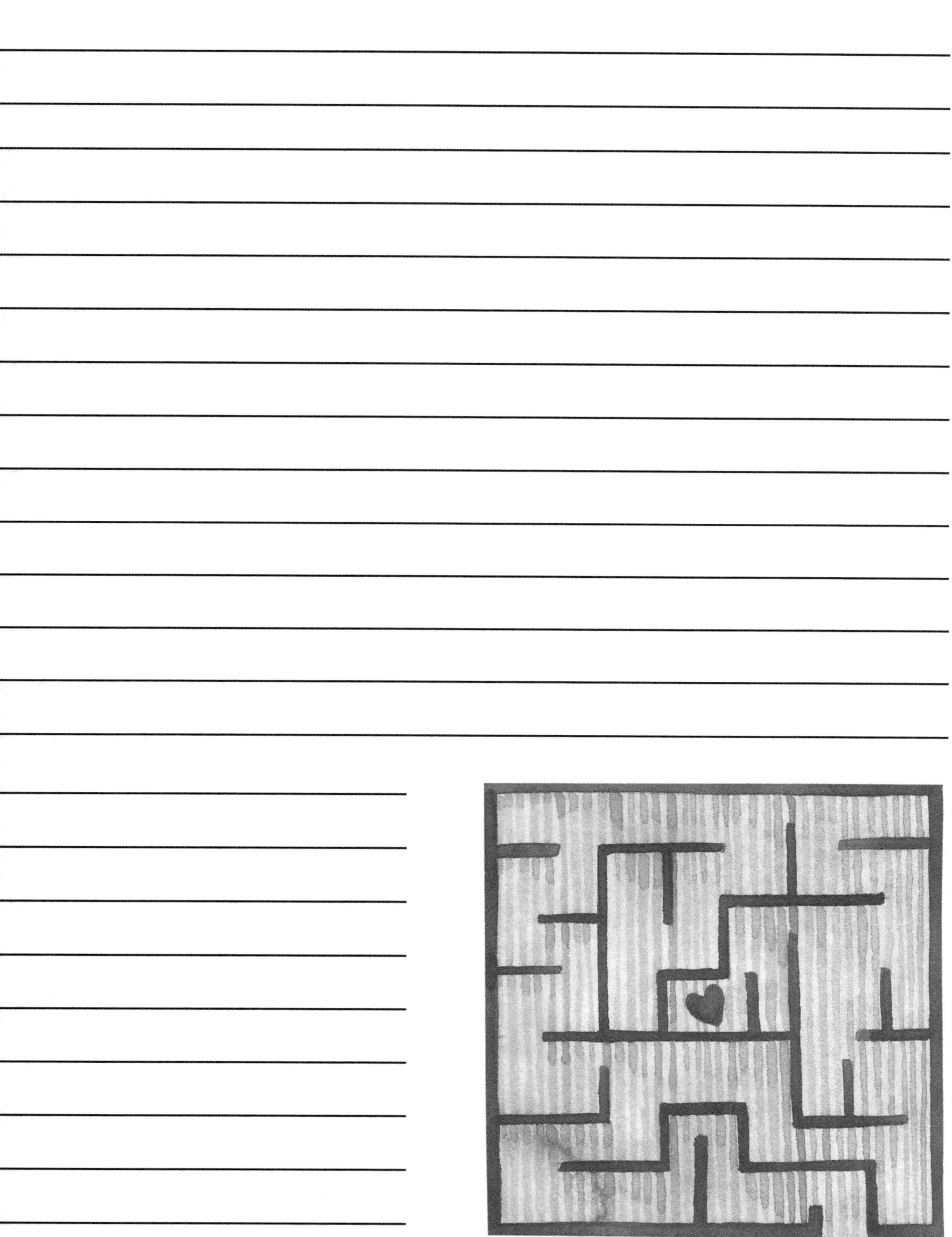

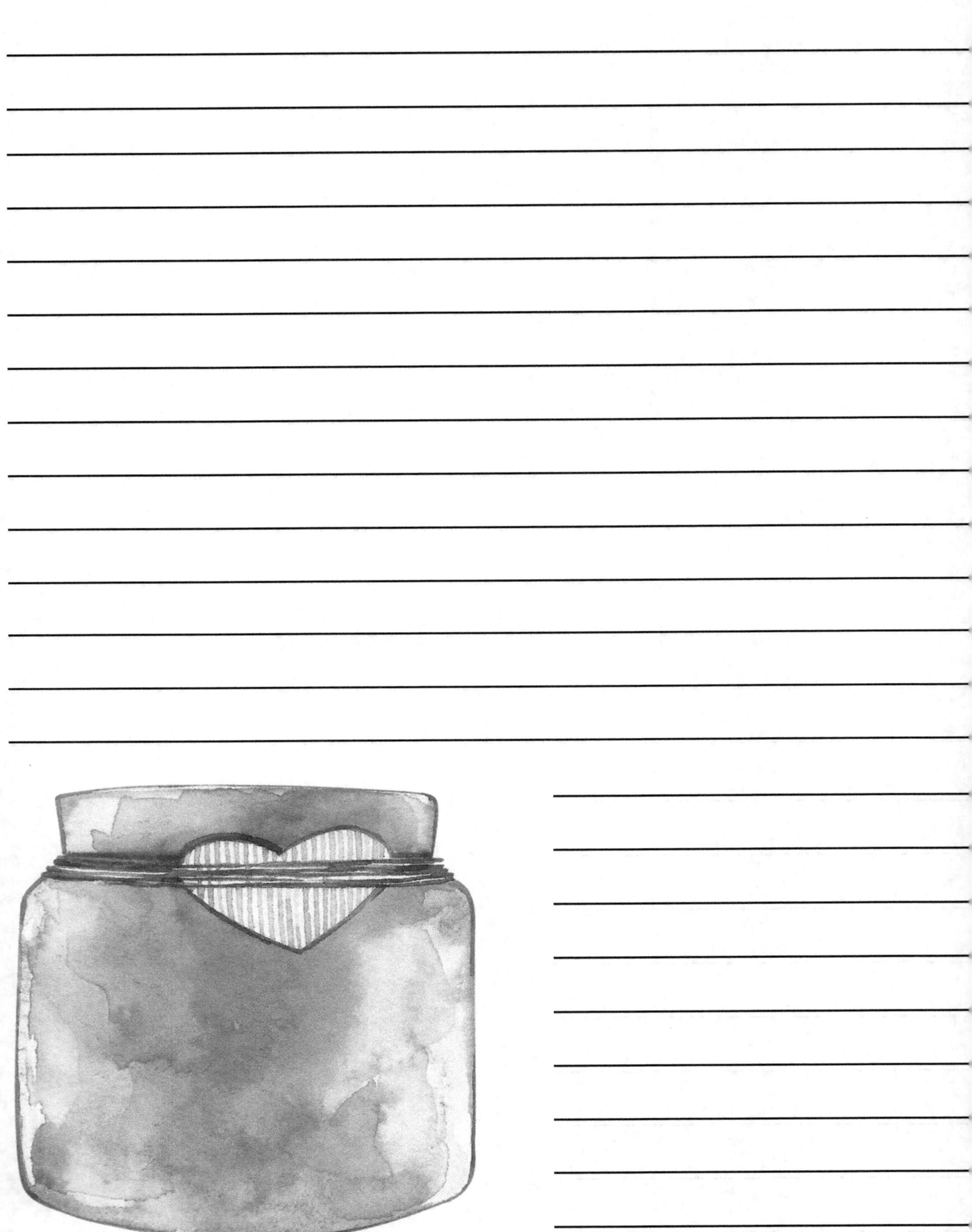

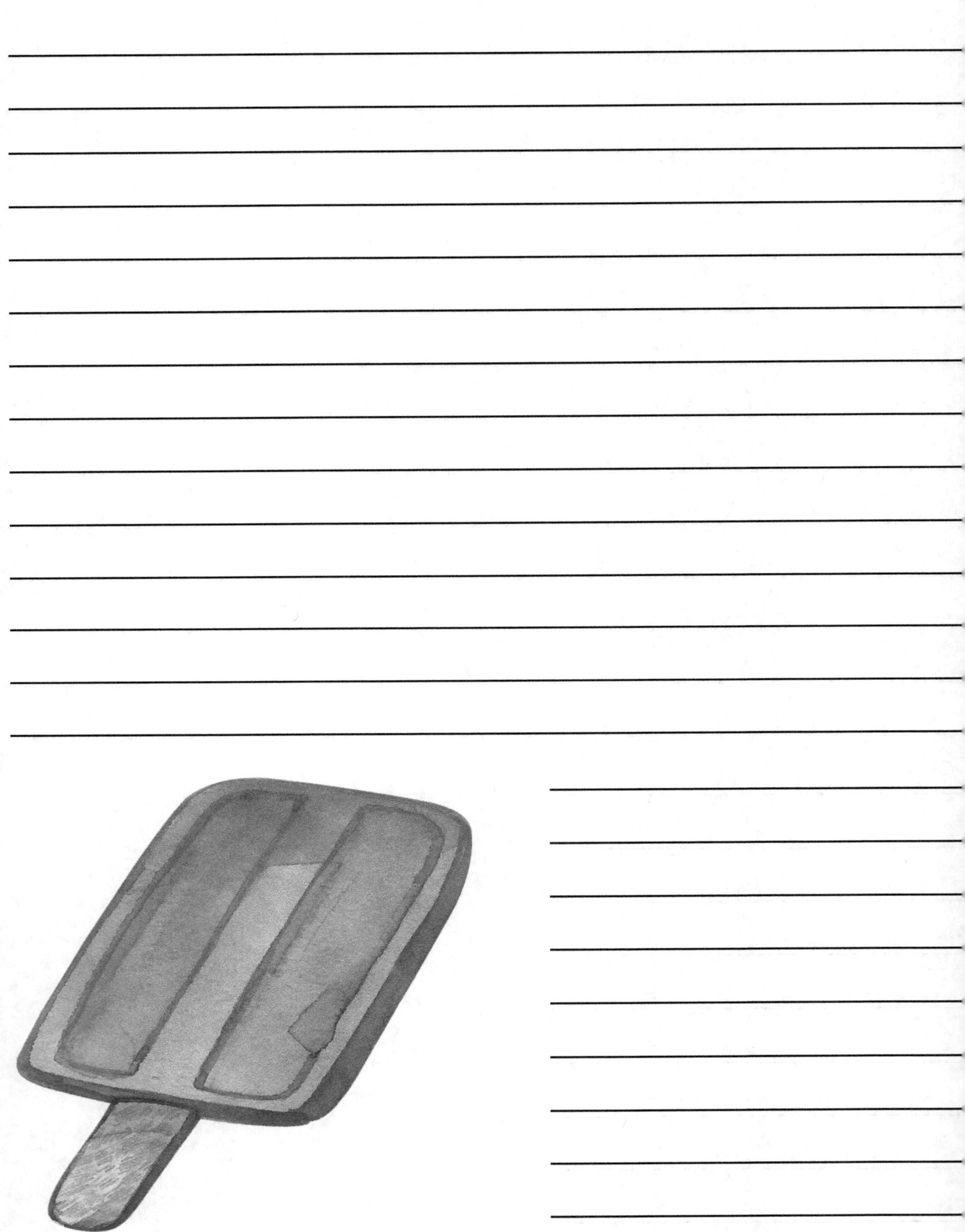

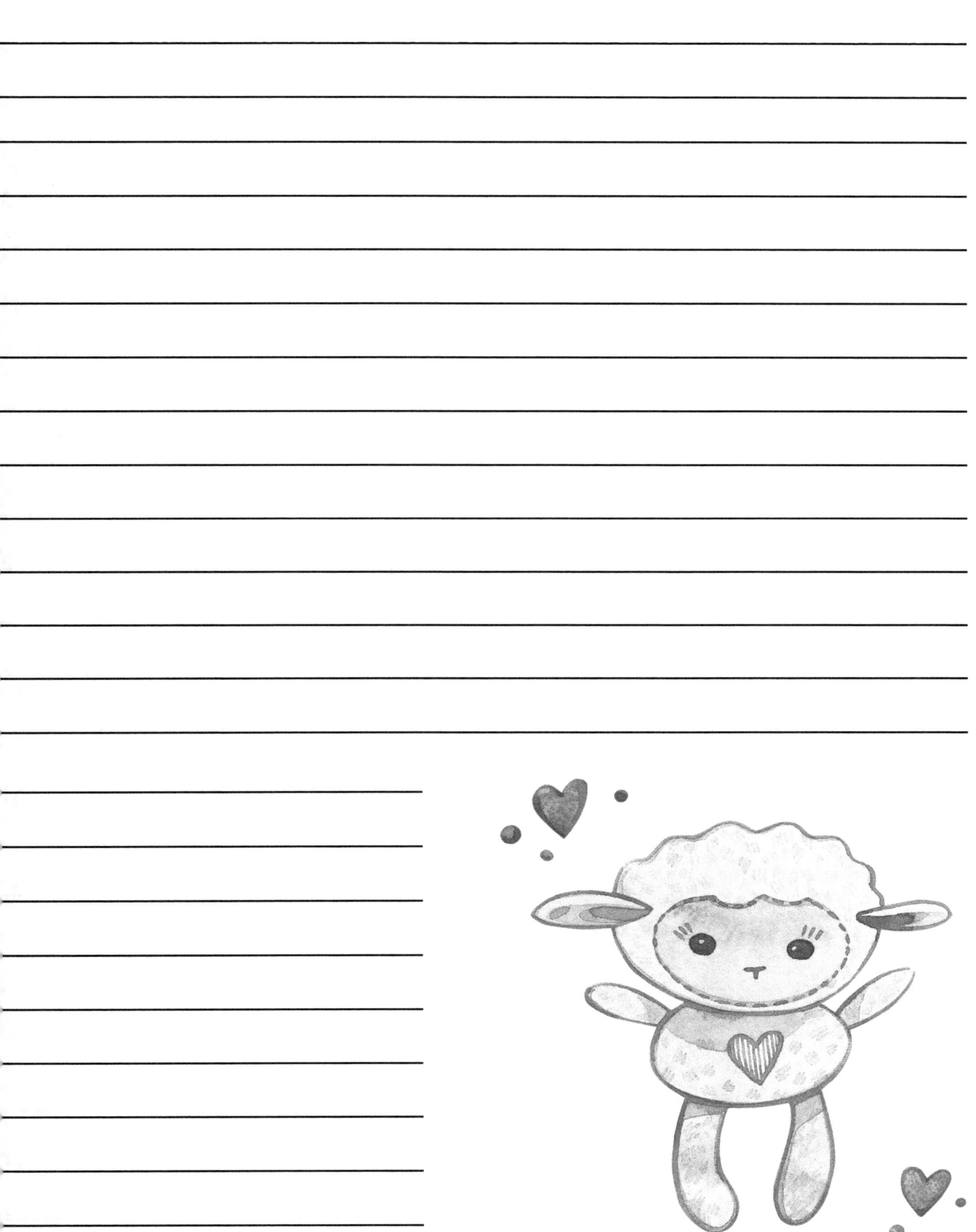

L
O
V
E

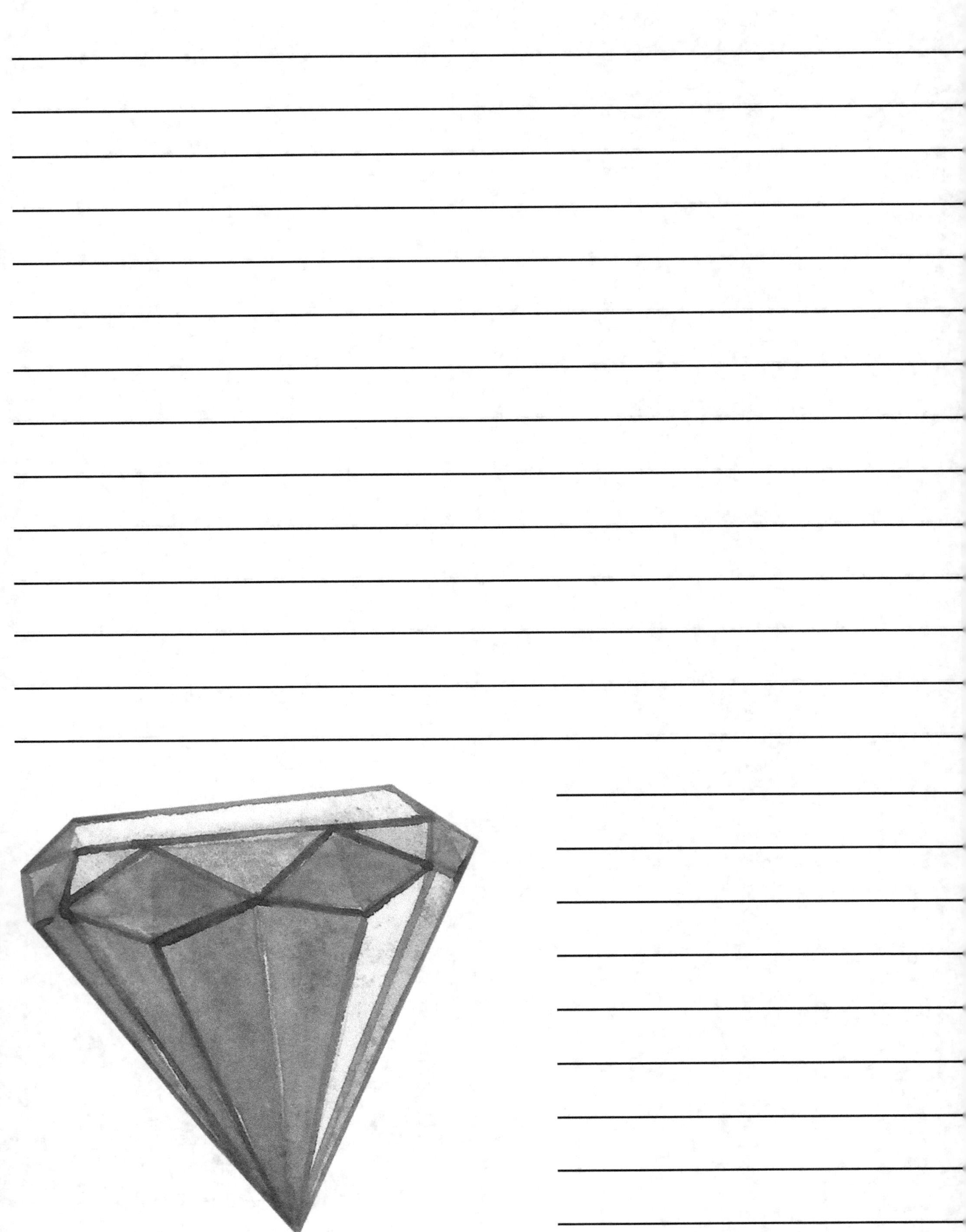

# - Acts of Kindness Tracker -

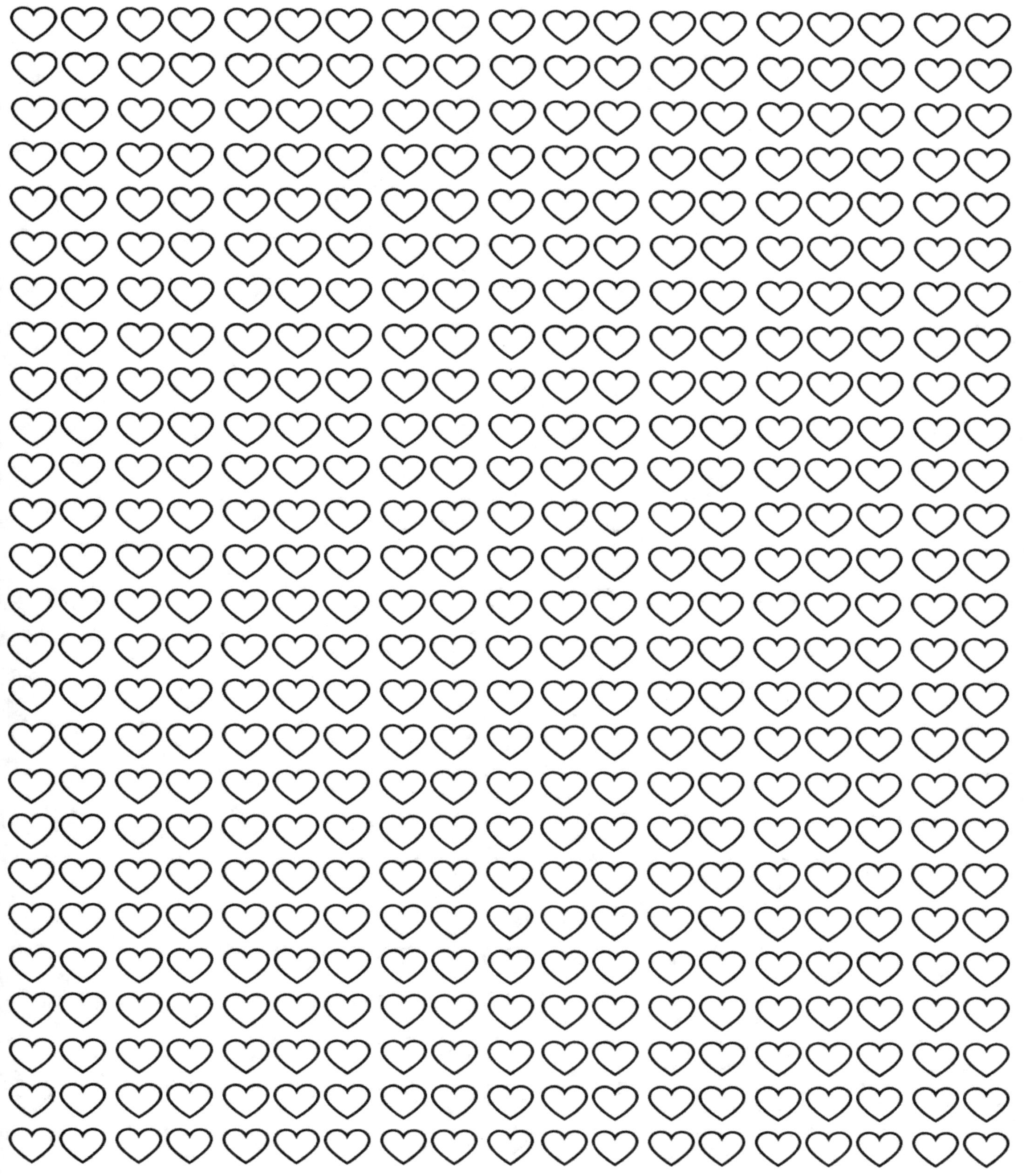

# - Acts of Kindness Tracker -

# - Acts of Kindness Tracker -

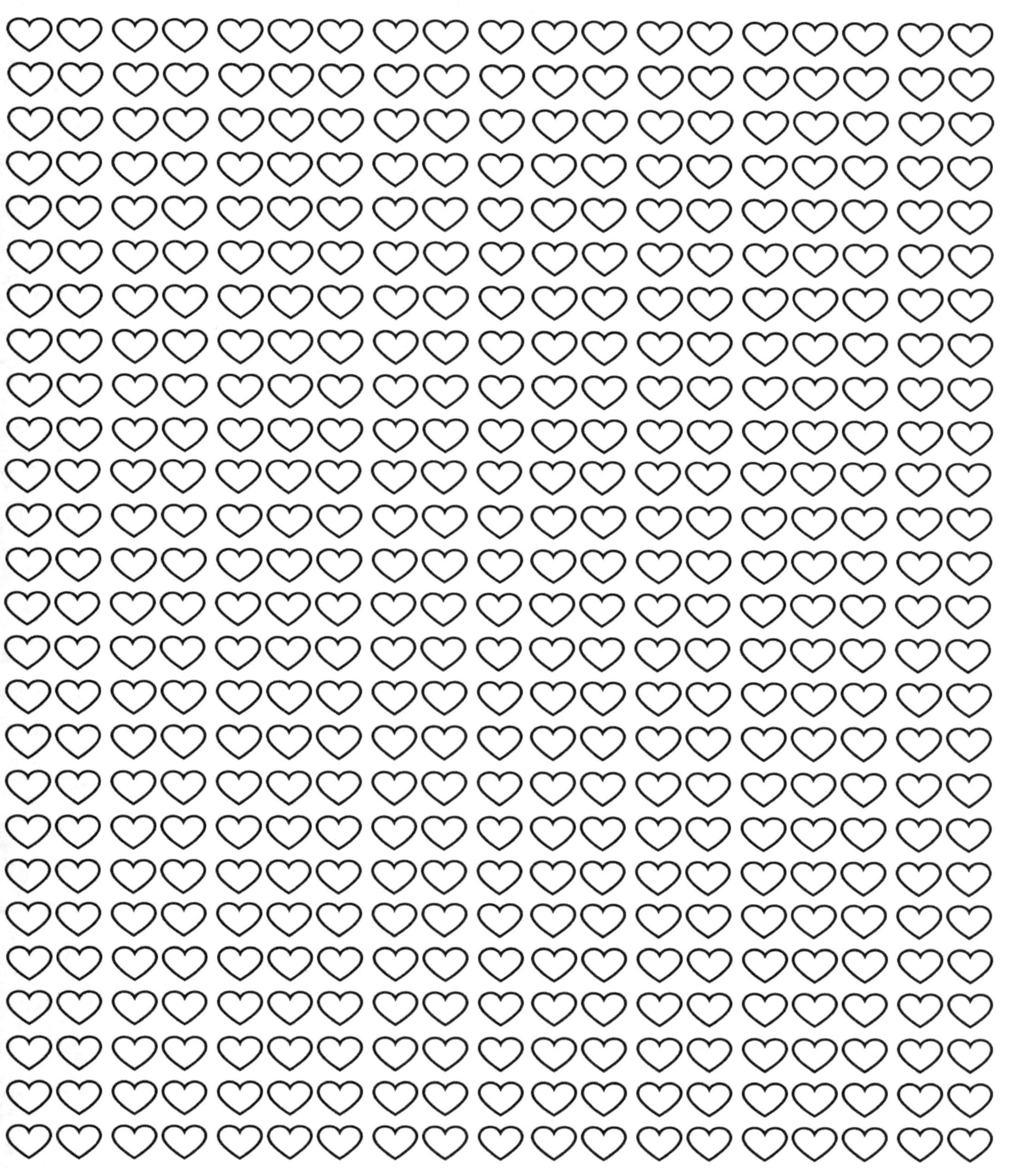

# Notes

# Notes

# Notes

www.ingramcontent.com/pod-product-compliance
Lightning Source LLC
La Vergne TN
LVHW080559200726
843510LV00004B/953

* 9 7 8 3 3 4 7 0 3 1 8 6 9 *